At Home in the Woodlands

James Alger

Illustrations by Julie Marie Marckel

Copyright © 2017 James Alger
All rights reserved.

ISBN-13: 978-1546538004
ISBN-10: 1546538003

To
JoAnn
Douglas
Julie
Stuart
Richard
who ventured with me
on my journey into the woods
for over half a century

Foreword

For half a decade, James Alger has journaled his regular forays into nature, closely observing the details of flora and fauna while reflecting upon the rhythms of constant change. His thoughtful, sensitive and vigorous writing — peppered with light-hearted stories and whims — stimulate muse in the reader. Recurring themes touch on discovery, spirituality, transformation, and coming to peace with inescapable laws of nature.

Part chronicle and part quest, "At Home in the Woodlands" is both timeless and timely as humanity's unending progression of cultural change and technological evolution turn our attention further and further from the essential elements of an Earth that sustains us. Joining Jim on this journey puts the reader in excellent company to refocus on our natural world and self-exploration.

— Kate Henne, Editor

Contents

1: Over the Dike 1

2: Shades of Blue and Brown 12

3: Snow and Fresh Footprints 63

4: The River Breaks Loose 127

5: The Birth of a Monarch Butterfly 173

6: Raspberry Season! 219

7: End of a Perfect Day 259

Chapter 1: Over the Dike

Sunday evening the family gathered for a Chinese dinner. We invited my grandnephew, Michael Hengel, and his dad, Chuck (who were "batching" it that day) to join us.

I'd been looking at some ducks that day, and the family informed me that 12-year-old Michael was an expert on ducks. I'd never been highly-educated on ducks, so that sounded intriguing to me — plus the fact that I had never really become acquainted with Michael before, as we lived quite a distance apart.

So, before we'd even served up our first rice and vegetables and said our prayers, I posed a question to Michael. I couldn't wait.

"Michael," I said, "I hear you have quite an interest in ducks."

"I doubt you'll be able to stump him," his dad chimed in.

"So," I said, "I need some information. Am I more likely to see a green-winged teal, or a blue-winged teal here in Minnetonka?"

He told me readily (and these were almost the first words he said since he came into the room) that I would see the blue-winged teal here, because the green-wing teal brooded further south.

I knew I'd have to use mnemonics or I wouldn't remember tomorrow morning which he had said. So I registered in my head that my blue eyes were seeing a blue-winged teal.

At the end of the meal, as Chuck and Michael asked to be excused and headed for the door, I stood up to help see out my young mentor. I said, "Michael, I have one more question for you." He not only turned around, he came back into the room.

"What would be," I asked, "the four most likely ducks I would see here on the ponds in Minnetonka?" Without hesitation he answered, "the mallard, the wood duck, the bufflehead, and the common merganser—and you would probably see the blue-winged teal, too." And he had hardly said another thing during the whole meal, while we grownups gassed on about all that we knew.

Ah! The wisdom of youth. The future of our globe is in good hands.

I often depend upon my son, Doug, to remember things. One day I was telling someone I was 81. And Doug said quietly from beside me, "You're 82, Pa — otherwise I was born a year before you were married."

"Oh, thanks, Doug."

Doug is my repository of information. His fifty-year-old strength is also mighty handy at the other end of a heavy load. Yes, it's in good hands, this globe.

I remark upon the ducks because I'd just been doing my "over-the-dike" that afternoon in Minnetonka, down by several of its many ponds. Hence, the ducks, which I have seen here or have seen coming through in their migration.

Now I should say a word about this "over-the-dike" business. We humans expand our language exponentially, and then contract it into a few syllables so that we don't run out of breath. We are unlike the birds, who confine themselves to a few kaks and hoots and whistles and screams (along with some absolutely gorgeous songs), and they get along just fine in communicating, thank you. But we are given to verbiage.

So, my "over-the-dike" refers to where I write — at least a lot of the time. I load up my pens and such, and head over the dike and down by the Red River to write.

You see, there was a time when the Red River claimed this valley around Fargo, North Dakota. Eleven months of the year during the last millennium or so, it flowed quietly within its banks. Then one month of the year, it stretched and yawned and spread itself over the Valley, which was its perfect right to do, before quietly returning to its river banks for the rest of the year.

Then along came the white man. He thought this would be a nice place to live, and build his homes, and stadiums, and high-rises and parking ramps. But he took umbrage at this annual spring stretching of the river. So he built a dike.

When the river climbed over the dike, he built the dike higher, until us poor fellows with pen and equipment in hand could hardly climb over without risk to life and limb. So we dug toe-holds in the dike, and thus managed to scale it safely. There is a certain idiocy here in this contention with the river, but I leave it to the readers to worry that out for themselves.

Now my "over-the-dike" is always done on Sunday afternoon, wherever I am in the world. All of life comes to a screeching halt and I depart with pen in hand and you don't see me for a couple of hours. And I am in utter bliss. I thank the Lord that I have been given the privilege of such a retreat.

My wife insists that it doesn't have to be on Sunday every week. Why couldn't it be on Monday or Saturday sometimes? And I stare at her uncomprehendingly. She is sure there is an obsession there somewhere.

It should be noted that all of this began in the vicinity of Leech Lake in central Minnesota. In fact, it could readily be said that the roots of the writing are embedded in the shores of Leech Lake, where we took our holiday every summer for a half century, even though the actual writing began a few years after we had moved our summer doings a few miles away to Ham Lake, near Akeley, Minnesota.

I supposed the roots of even the Leech Lake experience reach back to my Scouting days in Morris, Minnesota, where I grew up. And I would venture to say that the roots of that lie with my father, Kenneth Alger, who was an excellent hunter and fisherman.

Dad had myself and my brother, Bob (my only sibling) out early in the morning, and at an early age, tramping the shelter belts to help flush pheasants. Or he took us out to sail mechanized model boats he had made with his own hands. And we loved it all.

I even heard it reported that he and Mother went camping on their honeymoon. And my wife and I did the same for our honeymoon.

What is it that pulls us humans, even as children, out of our walled-in enclosures to the out-of-doors? I suppose that pull happens because that's where we were before we learned how to build such enclosures, when the world was dangerous, and we were prey to predators.

However, we were always curious, and always wanting to wander outside of the security of our ancient campfires, which was sometimes our undoing, but also cause for our growth and development. We learned to build enclosures and dikes to hem ourselves in and increase our sense of security. And we built bigger and finer enclosures, and even castles in the air.

Yet ultimately, I believe all of this effort was disappointing. Enclosures were always static. The out-of-doors was always happening. It was always, always happening. Invariably. Constant in its constancy. And as often as I would try to contain it — like our attempts to contain the Red River — it would always slip from my grasp. And because it was so, it was always exciting. And beautiful.

Two major locations are the scenes of the writing here, the banks of the Red River of the North between Fargo and Moorhead, Minnesota, and the woods near Ham Lake, ten miles west of Walker, Minnesota and Leech Lake, the latter location in the summer and the former the rest of the year.

The other locations are wherever I happen to be on a Sunday afternoon: Minnetonka, the banks of the Mississippi, Los Angeles, the Yukon, the Black Forest of southern Germany, the bonny hills of Scotland. The location may not be constant. The one constant is the hour.

Artists have frequently tried to depict an image of the irresistible force meeting the immovable object. The sea and the cliff is a favorite image. I have seen that same image depicted in Western art and Oriental art.

The image suggests nature grinding away at itself. The sheer force of it intrigues me.

One could see that image even on the beaches of Leech Lake, where we summered year after year. Live by the beach and it will teach you this image again and again.

For example, why do we not have more fear of the occasional piece of broken glass that might fall into the lake where the children are swimming? On a few occasions I found such a piece, worn smooth and harmless as a rounded stone by the constant, hour-by-hour, day-by-day, year-by-year chaffing of sand against stone or glass by the pounding surf driven by the northwest winds blown in upon Templar Point there on the lake. Or consider the time that the lake turned over in the summer and the small fish, the tullibee, died by the thousands. We had never seen the like before or since.

Hordes of them washed up upon that same beach on Templar Point and lay rotting there in the hot summer sun. We raked them into three huge piles, estimating 500 of them in each pile.

There was nothing to do but dig a big hole in the sand beside each pile and push the carcasses in and cover them up with sand. We hoped the dog would not get at them and dig them up. We figured the place would reek with the stench the rest of the summer.

Quite the opposite was true. Within weeks (perhaps days, if we had checked) we could dig down and find absolutely no trace of them. The inexorable had met the unmovable.

That little spot on the shores of Leech Lake was a source of unending wonder. We seemed to discover something new there every summer.

The place was a little triangle of land, bound on each side by a steep hill, the two hills curving back away from the lake and joining each other perhaps a hundred yards back from the beach. It proved to be an idyllic spot. I even found the poison ivy was a blessing, which I will explain.

The first day we arrived and came down the hill, we were met by a sea of poison ivy as far as we could see. It was a challenge.

Being the only one in boots and long trousers, I was commissioned to carry piggy-back one-by-one my wife, JoAnn, and each of our four children across the sea of ivy to the safety of the beach. Once that was accomplished, I took long ropes and cordoned off the beach and a single cleared path that led to the back of the lot.

We had already determined that we were going to live out of doors in tents, so now we began the task of clearing the poison ivy for tent sites and walking paths that would keep the children safely away from the pesky plant. That took a little imagination.

The lot was almost entirely made up of loose sand and hummus. We found that the ivy grew in long stringers just a few inches under the ground. One could pull up long stringers of the plant in one pull, and tote it off out of the way.

I found that by moving the axe yard frequently, I could trample down new areas and beat out the ivy in that way. We also did some spraying. However, I say we took out "some" of the ivy. There was good reason for that.

The ivy helped to keep people, visitors, relatives, and family, confined to paths. We figured that in 50 years we would have trampled that little plot of land into dust.

As it was, those little havens of ivy became the places where bluebells, iris, and anemone graced the land, gave us years of enjoyment, and were never trampled by careless campers.

All those years we leased the land from the Ojibwe. They finally asked us to leave, because they wanted the land for themselves. We believed in their cause. We did not begrudge them the taking back of the land. We moved to Ham Lake nearby.

We have learned a lot of lessons from Nature, and we are grateful for that. I hope we have learned enough to give back to the planet as it has given to us in our sojourn here.

Sometimes the woods have been exacting, and even severe. I always felt that was because of mistakes we had made or warnings that we had not heeded. They were a stern teacher, and we have learned many lessons to our benefit.

But often times the woods have been a haven and a refuge and a retreat and an Eden of breathless beauty. The lifelong memory of it makes my eyes water.

What is written in the pages that lie ahead represents a journey that I have taken, a journey that I would invite you to take with me. It is not a journey of fourscore years, but a journey of a half decade inspired by weekly nature columns I have written for the Pilot Independent newspaper of Walker, Minnesota, and its editor Dean Morrill.

It has been a journey to explore more deeply what I have visited fleetingly in the midst of the to-and-fro of a working life. It has become an old saw that we humans rarely take time to stop and smell the roses, but I expect it's true. You can answer that best for yourself.

The format of the seasons is, I hope, not so familiar that it is trite, but I use it here as a comfortable path of which, at least those of us in the North, never tire. I am indebted to my editor Kate Henne for walking with me through the laborious process of sifting, and sorting, and adjusting, and constructing the shape and thrust of this book.

Of course the theme of change will be paramount. We all experience that, some more radically than others.

A half dozen other themes surface as I reconsider what I've written here. A few of them mean the most to me, and I am hoping the writing will bear them out.

One of them is the rapturous beauty the woods give to us, very much like a Max Reinhart setting for an opera of centuries ago, where the curtains are opened and we are overwhelmed by the beauty and splendor of the set, before we hear the first note of a singer. I've discovered that I must give a little time to the endeavor to really experience the beauty of the woods. The woods are very much like a timid kitten, who lurks around the corner a bit until he gets used to you, before he rushes out and leaps into your lap to be enjoyed.

The woods are like a kaleidoscope. Due to weather and light changes they offer beauty in many different ways.

You will find other themes here as well. What I call "cosms," for one theme — microcosms and macrocosms — seeing big things in little things and the like.

Also there is the "making sense" that humans do, the "filling-in the gaps," where we don't quite understand. Sometimes we can't even see what we fill in.

What is universal for all of us is that we all pass on. I often have heartfelt feeling about this as I sit in the woods and let the woods seep into me.

Year by year, month by month, day by day — and even moment by moment — the woods are changing around me. If only I could sense the change as if it were a living thing.

I came to the woods by Ham Lake long ago as an older teenager. I camped with my father and three other deer hunters in this very place.

There is very little that I recall about that experience, except that we had a campfire, and the men told stories — mostly comic anecdotes, some of them a bit bawdy, as I recall. I just remember being surrounded by great Norway pines.

Now as I sit in this same place among tall Norway pines I realize that probably none of these trees has an age that reaches back to 1948. All of those that surrounded me then are dead and gone.

It is a new forest. Everything has changed. And yet it is as if nothing has changed. Perhaps a few of these were young saplings then. Perhaps they too remember the great giants of 1948.

Chapter 2: Shades of Blue and Brown

As I sit down to enjoy the woods in the closing days of summer, I look ahead to how the autumn will develop as the woodland transforms itself toward the day when it first takes on the cloak of winter. It is a sometimes peaceful and sometimes stormy period, as if the peace were meant to remind us of the repose of summer and the storm to prepare us for the rigors of winter.

One can imagine these days, not because we can see into the future, but because we can remember past autumns. The woods offer no hard and fast promise that this autumn will be the same as those past, but humans have grown accustomed to seeing the past as a promise of sorts, and respond accordingly.

If I heat my home with wood, and I know that it takes seven cords of wood to heat my home until warm weather comes again, then autumn is the season when I take out my axe and saw and head for my woodlot to prepare firewood for winter. And over time I have learned that a ten-acre plot of fast-growing softwood can replenish itself fast enough to heat my home perpetually.

The mellowness of late summer has descended upon the woods, like the threadbare mantel laid gently onto the shoulders of an aging man. The white oaks have started to show some yellowing leaves. A brown leaf dangles, twirling under an alder branch, seemingly suspended in mid-air. Likely it is hanging from the threads of some spider webbing.

A kind of hush seems to hang upon the land, as if the deep woods are waiting for something. They have done their germinating, procreating, flowering, fruiting and maturing. Now they seem to be waiting for whatever might next be in store.

The woods seem to have paused, quieter now than in midsummer, as if to hold a kind of reverent silence before the close of the year. Today I hear chickadees, but otherwise silence.

The small raspberry plant (I can hardly call it a bush, as it's so small) that I've been observing since this spring has grown from eight to ten inches, and it looks as if that is all it plans to do for this season. It lacks much sunshine here in the woods; no doubt it would do much better in an open meadow. Yet its habitat is here as well, for it has many cousins about it here on the forest floor.

How much one feels in the north country that a full season (spring, summer and fall) is like a full cycle of life. We know that it isn't, for it is only another year in the lives of all the plants and animals around us.

Yet it seems like everything around us in a season is born, grows, matures and dies within that time, with the single peculiarity that most have a resurrection when they will burst forth, alive to enjoy another season. Even my small raspberry plant, which has started to show some yellow leaves, will come back to grace this woodland in another year.

The forest colors have started to change, particularly some of the early changers, like the birches. It is interesting to note that the tall deciduous trees that are exposed to the wind and sun have changed, while the smaller ones in the deep woods are still green.

The poplar leaves all around me are a curious creation. Their thin, flat stems enable them to twist almost 180 degrees in the breeze. They are the woodland's glitter, catching the eye like the dance-hall girl's glitter on her sparkling gown. The little round leaves are shaped like a paddle, and made to catch the breeze like a propeller, so that when the breeze comes, you can quickly spot every poplar around you from all the other leaves in the forest. The quaking aspen dances like this, and I must see if I can distinguish the aspen from our common poplar.

The bird activity delights me here on this late afternoon, as I'm surprised to see this much activity this late in the year. I hadn't even had a chance to unfold my woolly lawn chair in the deep, colorful autumn woods, when a dark brown bird darted among some bushes at eye level about 20 feet in front of me.

At first he wouldn't reveal himself so I could identify him. Then he flew quickly behind the bole of a large poplar tree.

A moment later a kingfisher made his presence known with his rattling sounds in the direction of the lake about 100 yards behind me. He kept circling around to my right until he was behind me, but he refused to let himself be seen. At last he flew directly over my head and dashed off toward Hay Lake, a few hundred yards to my left.

No sooner had kingfisher disappeared than a green heron announced his presence with his resonant pumping sound. He flew into some pines and stayed there for some time, sounding away; but he would not let me see him. At last he flew away, and I spotted his dark body with its flashes of white.

Ah! Some geese betray their presence as they fly overhead behind me. The geese do not let me see them behind the trees but their signature honking announces their presence. It is that season again; the season for hunters. I chatted with a couple of bow hunters the other day, and they reminded me that bow hunting will open soon.

The white-breasted nuthatch announces himself with his double-noted "too-too" to my left and behind me a little. But he remains out of sight. Perhaps he'll make an appearance while I'm here. A downy woodpecker hammers a few whacks on a nearby pine tree, and then flies off.

A house fly takes an extraordinary interest in the back of my hand. He's not easily intimidated. When I push him with the end of my pen, he just jumps up a few inches and then settles back for a further check. Then a tinier-than-usual mosquito lands on my other hand and checks me out, but flies away unfed.

A gray squirrel descends a tall poplar to my right. Where did he come from? He's not 10 feet from me. He eyes me nervously, circles the tree trunk a few times, jumps to the ground and then up onto a long old fallen poplar. I think, "Ah, now I can engage him, for I've put some pieces of pancake onto that log." But he runs the length of the log, hops blithely over my dainty morsels and runs off into the woods. Not his cup of tea, I guess.

A moment later, a tan feral baby cat (we have a number of them proliferating in these parts now) appears, slinking through the woods from my left. He eyes me a bit, and then heads for the pancakes. He's hungry, and he's not fussy. Now he slinks off into the woods.

The woods will be strutting their colors throughout this time of year. I never cease to marvel at this annual display. The red oaks, with their spike-pointed leaves, will develop a brilliant red that is iridescent in the afternoon sun down by the lake.

Something about the fall colors continues to intrigue me from year to year, and draws me forth at least once each fall to walk among them when they are most beautiful.

How the fall colors stun us, even the early changers. JoAnn took a walk in the woods when we were over near Akeley last weekend to gather some small branches of oak and maple. She described a color setting that I simply had to go and see.

When we came upon it, it took my breath away. It was a sea of glistening red sumac, glowing in the bright sunlight and in the midst of it, a single blue aster.

The birches by the lake take their time donning their autumn apparel, and are just starting to take on their yellow. These brilliantly-colored autumn leaves strike me as a strange phenomenon. I want to pick and preserve them to admire them later, but they disappear on me. They are like ghosts.

Why do the pigments in the lovely leaves dissolve? Is color so ephemeral?

Perhaps Nature is teaching me in her quiet way that any breathtaking moment I experience in the deep woods must be drunk to the lees, for I shall never taste it again, nor shall any other human being. And perhaps that is why the sages tell us to take time to smell the roses.

I am like [the Apostle] Peter, who viewed the Transfiguration and wanted to build three booths for Jesus, Moses and Elijah, to preserve the moment. But it could not be done.

******

Each year as summer begins to close, we pack a trailer full of things we'll need to take back to our winter home, and make our first trip back to Fargo. This morning finds me on the banks of the Red River, which runs through Fargo near our home.

The woods here treat me to Harris sparrows, apparently passing through on their migration south. They light in a small bush near the river bank, 20 feet in front of me, so I have a good opportunity to observe them. Several spend all their time preening in the morning sun.

And now to complete my birding day, three whistling swans pass overhead. With their low crooning tones, they signal the end of another day.

How different the dance of the leaves in the autumn breeze. The great cottonwood in the autumn ripples at the world around it like the quaking aspen did in midsummer.

I have just surprised a young Lab, who has come bounding into the weeds off his owner's leash. He shows the usual Lab friendliness, snorting a bit but not barking. He nuzzles me a little, decides I fit and goes bounding off, his master frantically chasing after him.

Meanwhile, the beginning autumn golds and russets of the cottonwood and a neighboring oak provide the proscenium for this marvelous parade, and a song sparrow is the organ master for this silent movie. The oak and cottonwood tilt and sway in the warm breeze, drawing attention to themselves as if to remind us that they, too, are important in the whole scheme and scene of things.

The giant willow (three feet in diameter at its base) swishes its leaves as if painting a masterpiece against the blue easel of the sky. The big elm behind me reaches its great limbs over me like an umbrella and dips and bows its yellow leaves and branches as if greeting some lordly monarch.

A small Skye terrier moves lazily across the large patch of blue sky in front of me. Of course, it is a fleecy patch of cumulus cloud. But how creative the vapors are in creating endless images for us.

Remember in our carefree youngest days, when we were only responsible for some chores and some growing up, we would go out into the open pasture under a lone cottonwood and stretch out contentedly to gaze up at that wonderfully deep blue late summer or autumn sky? And nature would march past us that splendid parade of fantastic cloud figures — animals, castles, bridges, small cars, great ocean liners.

Now the Skye terrier cloud moves lazily off to the south, almost out of my sight. He has stretched himself into a dachshund, and the wisp of him waves at me as he disappears behind the trees.

It seems that nature's imagination is endless, and she (ah, yes, nature is the great feminine that nurtures and nourishes and mothers us, while she nestles us gently in her arms) can always create the cloud images that we recognize. She makes the show just for us.

The strato-cumulus clouds eventually stretch themselves from horizon to horizon, like long rolls of white and gray cotton, accented by the blue sky behind them. The entire mass moves slowly north. I can only detect their movement at all by their passage behind a tall willow in front of me.

The cloud rolls disguise the approaching sunset behind me, but they betray the evidence of that sunset by tinting beautifully the white cottony edges of each roll with a bright pink. The waning glow of the pink announces the setting of the sun. Gradually the glow fades to a suggestion of a rose color.

A lone Canada goose flies leisurely by, high overhead. He would go by unnoticed, were it not for the fact that he heralds his flight with constant honking. Stealth is certainly not a description you would attach to a goose.

A small fish makes an equally-small jump in the center of the Red River in front of me, apparently snatching the morsel of a small insect that landed for a moment on the river's surface. I say a small jump, for the fish barely broke the surface, leaving a ring of evidence widening after him. The river moves lazily after a long drought.

The riparian area along the river is lush and green. The brome grass offers lush cover over the whole area. A burgeoning cluster of green stands four feet tall behind me. It looks to me like a woodbine, but I must look further into its identity.

A small ash I have observed for two years seems to be progressing. It stands nine feet tall now, just over my reach. This small tree has survived two floods this spring and early summer; the first with ice and the second, without. He is a stout fellow.

Three slate-colored juncos flit about and then disappear into a clump of green ash trees along the river bank by the Red River. The ash are a low group of sprouts or saplings that appear more like a bush than a tree, the tallest part reaching up perhaps 18 feet. They grow from an old ash stump, the surviving part of a larger ash tree dating back long ago, before I can remember it.

The old ash was perched right on the river bank and must have endured severe beatings from ice and floods before it succumbed. But it left these sprouts as a remembrance that it once stood here.

These gyrations that the juncos do before they land in the ash clump — what is that all about? It is like an aerial dance. It is almost as if they are sporting about to see who will dive first into the brush cover, and then one suddenly takes the lead and others follow.

This small area is a kind of microcosm of the entire forest floor. The abundance of species here is overwhelming. It is as if nature said, "We will cast the seeds of a thousand species on this spot on the globe." Nature is profligate in that regard.

How do these species serve one another? The trees like this ash, and the great trees, of course, provide shade and shelter for cool growth. But perhaps each species, besides the trees, serves its neighbors in some way.

Since the area all around is devoid of small trees, I truly did not expect this young ash would survive two years of ice and floods. Perhaps he will live to join the giant elm behind me and the giant willow to my left, and the giant oak far to my right; and I will sit under him in his shade one day.

The sky offers a complete overcast of strato-cumulus clouds here by the Red River, but no rain disturbs me yet, as I sit among the tall vegetation in the river woods. Everything is a fresh green yet. A flock of several dozen Canada geese pass overhead, headed south.

Now several yellow throats appear to my left in the tall grass about 40 feet away. They dive into the grass, appear briefly with the flash of yellow on their heads, and then dive into the grass again, after their breakfast. Bird man Roger Tory Peterson tells us they frequent low vegetation in swamps, stream beds, marshes and clearings, such as we have here.

A group of young Harris' sparrows cavort around in an old dead ash tree about 30 feet in front of me. They are nervous little fellows, seeming barely able to sit still for a moment. They flash the white patch on their front, unlike the mature bird.

Great beads of water cling to the narrow leaves of the brome grass all around me, standing out like strings of brilliant pearls on the green throat of the grass. Yesterday saw a heavy downpour of rain most of the day, much appreciated by almost everyone after the long drought months. Almost everyone — except, perhaps, truck gardeners trying to get into muddy fields after their produce.

A tall common hackberry tree has taken a beating in the wind, where it stands some distance to my right. A long heavy limb, freshly broken off, lies on the ground. It was once actually the stem of the tall central trunk that reached up above it. Its loss leaves the tree looking forlorn at the top, but it still sports a number of big, healthy limbs below. The broken stem has a green cluster at the top with red berries in it, which is fed only by a single strand of live bark that reaches up one side of an otherwise dead stem.

How vigorously it shows its efforts at survival!

The Red River of the North moves lazily but inexorably north past me on its journey from Lake Traverse to — well, the sea, eventually. As ancient as the river is, the water before me is the same only for a moment, and then it flows past to the north and disappears from my view forever;

unless, of course, it passes into the clouds and returns one day as rain. But the accurate knowledge of that is too large and mysterious for my understanding.

I've often wondered how much water in this river flows by me per second. The other day in the news a riverologist informed us about that very matter. He said not to be deceived when the river is low. It is still flowing so rapidly, if you will notice, that a very heavy rainfall could make it flood again immediately. It flows by now at 2,000 cubic feet per second. Normal flow at this time of year is 250 cubic feet per second. There you have it.

Even as I watch the trees change from moment to moment by dropping now one leaf, then another, I see the river change before me. It seems to travel slowly, as it has for tens of thousands of years. But at times when the Red River is swollen from extensive fall rains, its swifter movement shows itself only when it carries a leaf or twig quickly by on its smooth surface, smooth, save for the spots where raindrops pock its surface.

In a wistful gesture, I toss a stick out into the middle of the stream. For many minutes I can watch a same patch of water as it bears my stick away until, at last, it disappears into the distance and into the mass of flowing water around it. While other parts of nature stand long enough for me to get a look at them, even the clouds, the river never does and always passes like a dream that you can never fall back asleep and dream again.

The river, we are told, was made by the advancing and retreating of a great ice sheet thousands of years ago. It has left this channel through which north-flowing waters have coursed for countless ages. The flora and fauna along its banks change from age to age and from year to year, and even from moment to moment. As important as we humans are, we are born and live and die and pass on downstream, as it were, like the leaf on the current, and disappear.

However the river keeps on coursing. There is something we love about a river that links us with the eternal.

I wonder if my readers remember a children's book from 60 years ago (if you admit to such an age) about an Ojibwe boy who lived along the waterway of the Great Lakes who carved a boat and paddler, named it "Paddle-to-the-Sea" and put it into the lake to travel seaward? My stick tossed upon the river made me think of that.

The story contains the feeling that we are a part of the flow of a great stream, like that patch of water on the Red River. But the stream is too large and mysterious for my mind to grasp the whole of it. The boy carver wrote on his carving, "I am 'Paddle-to-the-Sea.' Please put me back in the water so I can go on."

A river teaches me something. There is a kind of flow to my life. Sometimes I am lifted from that flow, when my life is interrupted. But in time I am put back into that flow and I move on, until finally I am emptied into the great Sea.

A small bee with yellow markings moves from blossom to blossom among the white asters that surround me as I sit by the Red River again. I can pick him up in my binoculars. He sports about in Bacchanalian revelry, drinking himself full of nectar of the gods. He checks out the Canadian thistle blossoms nearby but they only offer brown husks of former blossoms of mid-summer. How well he deserves the description attached to him of "busy." Will he and his companions continue this activity for several hours as I sit among them?

He has a noted namesake among us humans in the Greek Aristotle, who was — oops! excuse me — Sophocles, who was known as the Attic Bee during his sojourn in Athens 300 years BCE. He gained this name, not only for the sweetness of his words, but also for his constant activity in that city.

The gray earth under my feet has a curious appearance. It looks like a honeycombed windshield that has just been struck by a great rock. Its clods are surprisingly uniform in size; rarely over eight inches across, and usually with more than four sides to them. Deep crevices separate them, in which the drying-out continues.

I have been trying for the last half hour to whistle in a small dark bird that flits among the tall grasses and weeds that stand as tall as I am sitting, but he refuses to show himself. His call is a light whistle, as he works the weeds and seeds, much like a housewife might hum to herself as she works her dough into delicious bread that she will bake until it makes ecstasy out of the air for anyone coming into her kitchen. But somehow this winged fellow near me now refuses to let himself be seen. Then suddenly he flits across a space too quickly to be seen well. Perhaps he is a wood peewee with his dark back and white breast.

This is the season of the migration of butterflies that move south in early autumn. I am seeing hardly any of them now, even in the grassy openings in the woods. Some months ago I remarked on an all-brown butterfly that landed on a tree near this very spot. It seemed like it blended into the brown bark of the oak on which it rested. On looking for some kind of identity for this lovely creature, the closest I could come is that it seemed to be one of the fritillaries, perhaps the regal fritillary, because of its size.

A ruffed grouse goes trekking by some distance from where I am sitting. I'm impressed with how small these little fellows are for a game bird. He darts forward, pauses to search the ground, perhaps for food, and then darts forward again. After a time he takes to the air for no apparent reason, then appears to settle down into the woods again after a short flight.

The small bees continue drawing nectar from the white asters around me. They are, indeed, as tireless as the river, to do what nature bids them do.

****

Now there's an experience! I'm standing on the riverbank, eyeing the far bank with my binoculars for any signs of life, as is my habit when I first arrive. The early sun is just topping the tree line above the far bank.

I scan from far right to far left, catching sight of nothing yet. I lower the glasses and just stand to enjoy the pristine look of the morning river, with beads of dew bejeweling everything.

The river seems almost still. Only when I spot a small stick moving slowly on the surface do I detect its flow and movement. Everything is quiet, except for the very faint call of a couple of geese in the distance behind me.

At Home in the Woodlands

Then suddenly out of the corner of my eye to the left I detect a rippling on the river surface that shouldn't be there. It comes right from under the river bank where I am standing. Whatever is disturbing the water is as yet out of sight but as the rippling becomes more pronounced, I know it is moving toward me.

Now it appears — the head of a large beaver toting a small cottonwood branch with some green leaves still on it, laboring upstream in the water with his load. Had he cut down a small cottonwood downstream and stripped some of its young branches for his engineering project upstream? Perhaps he's making winter quarters.

I stand right on the brink of the river bank, four feet above the surface of the water. If I'm careful, the beaver will pass directly below me. Were I to move, he would thwack the water with his leathery tail, disappear under the water and my experience with him would be at an end.

I freeze, and he pulls his awkward load near me. When he is directly below me, he halts in the shallow water. For several haunting moments, he eyes me with one eye to see if I will move or if I offer any danger. I hold my breath. Then he moves on. All this while, he is practically soundless.

As I turn back toward my woolly chair, a Savannah sparrow greets me among the tall weeds, with his streaked breast and the faintest suggestion of a yellow hue in his markings. The weeds and grasses stand as high as eye level to me. The sparrow sports about among the tall weeds, plucking seeds as he goes, giving me time to get a good look. He is on his migration south. In another week or two, he will be gone.

The tobacco weed is so-called because in autumn, it turns the dark brown of harvested tobacco. The plants around me are still in their summer green and quite attractive. They stretch up 44 inches, and I sit at about 42 inches. But some of the more exuberant ones nearby reach up four and five feet toward the blue sky. Sprinkled plentifully among them are the white wood asters. At a little distance, I can see three or four of the tobacco weeds have already turned their handsome autumn brown. So I am surrounded by quite an attractive array of flora.

A flicker has been circling me from one tree to another, flashing his showy red cockade. He fusses among bunches of brown leaves, no doubt after lunch of some kind.

A few humans are busy across the Red River from where I sit. They are mowing down the flora to make beautiful parkland, so they don't have to sit, chin-deep, among the asters and wheat grass (Sigh!) No doubt I'm not good for our flagging economy. If everyone did as I am doing, there wouldn't be much sale of riding lawn mowers.

I have some allergies, but the plants about me seem to be kind to me so far. We'll see how long I'll be able to last. I see some woodbine and thistle at a distance, but no ragweed or goldenrod. Perhaps the prime pollen season hasn't arrived yet.

The white asters that surround me have taken on their autumn vestments. Their white blossoms have completely disappeared and have been replaced by the little white cotton balls that contain their seeds. The tiny white wood aster has set aside its blossoms in favor of the feathery ball of seed clusters, preparing to scatter the seeds of its lineage upon the ground to give birth to a new generation next spring.

The little feathery ball looks very much like a tiny version of the white seed cluster of the dandelion after it has gone to seed. I take one of the tiny feathery balls off its stem and lay it gently on the lap board that lies across the arms of my lawn chair, where I sit hemmed in on all sides by wheat grass, Canada thistles and wood asters on this absolutely-gorgeous October day. When I begin to take it apart, it immediately disintegrates into a tiny feather bed of softness.

How profligate nature is in seed-making. I count perhaps 40 seeds in the little feather ball. Then I count perhaps 20 such feather balls on each branch of the plant, and 10 branches on each plant. We've already figured 8,000 seeds on one plant, and I look about at a sea of asters in all directions, beyond my ability to count.

Of course, in addition to making a new generation of plants, they are good for birds and small mammals. But still, how many they number! Their species will surely survive.

A few weeks ago, I took a special interest in the wheat grass that I see all about, standing about 40 inches high. Some folks have nicknamed it "wheat weed."

I broke off a full stem at the ground, being careful not to disturb the root, and sent it to David Osheim, an Iowa relative who is an agronomist at Iowa State University in Ames. He checked with a plant expert who identified it as intermediate wheat grass.

I asked if it was called intermediate because it was halfway between domestic and wild, but there was no answer to that. It is found in the Dakotas and Montana, but not in Iowa.

A light breeze whisks the aster seeds off my desk board. It's time for them to begin a new generation and for me to bid them farewell.

I see a few cockleburs near me. The moment I mention cockleburs, you likely summon up nasty experiences you've had picking them out of your wool socks, and you wonder how anyone in their right mind could choose to sit among them. I can sympathize with you, because I've had those experiences, too.

The big plant with many burs stands more than 40 inches tall, higher than my head where I am sitting. Its branches reach over near my lap board, so that I can easily reach out, pick one of the burs, and set it on my board in front of me. Surprisingly, its little spines are soft to the touch, not harsh like the spines of my cactus plants at home. True, when I touch it to my wool jacket, it sticks.

But I remind myself it is only doing its proliferating thing and asks for a ride a little distance, until it falls off, or I take it off, where it can start a new generation.

Again I am impressed with what a spendthrift and how imaginative nature is in producing seed to replace its plants. Nature is lolling into the last stages of this autumn season.

I have pondered this proliferation at some length now, and I leave myself a bit puzzled as to why I do all this pondering. Obviously it intrigues me.

There must be some design in all of this seemingly generous regeneration, this super-abundant making of seeds and offspring. By this I am not alluding to a theological discussion of the Great Designer. That might be the subject of a whole other writing.

Here I am only referring to the "design" of nature. A lot goes through my head at this point, which might make food for discussion at another time. But to cut a very long discussion very short, it is likely survival that nature is aiming at. That answers only the "what," not the "why," but let us leave it at that for now.

A barred owl hoots at me, with his distinct four hoots in a certain rhythm. The overcast clouds make it a gray day, and the evening is settling in even earlier than October dictates. So my owl friend is heralding the night a bit earlier than usual.

As evening approaches, a surprising amount of bird activity entertains me, compared to a warm midday when things are often pretty quiet in the bird world. Very likely they are about a bit of feed before settling in for the night. A woodpecker, perhaps a downy, whangs away on the big white oak tree behind me. He doesn't have the courtesy to come out front where I can get a good look at him.

A couple of chickadees chitter about in the willow in front of me, no doubt having a last snack before bedtime. One just about took my cap off flying over me. He veered off as if to say, "What are you doing, sitting there?"

As the dusk settles, the yellow of the intermediate wheatgrass catches the last of the evening light and reflects it. And for those of you who like to do a little name-dropping among friends, it is called *thimopyin intermedium*.

How still the woods are on an autumn evening. The oaks and birch that had leaves have spread them in a brown carpet on the forest floor. Only the quietness remains, as the evening settles in around me

A small oak nearby, not six feet high, has clung to one last big, brown leaf of summer, a leaf as big as those that had graced its bigger partners who reached up more than 60 feet into the sky, as if to say, "I can grow them as big as you and cling to my last one even longer than you!"

A flock of 12 Canada geese fly over me in perfect formation now, headed south. Soon another flock of 15 comes after them, noisily in ragged formation. All things are preparing themselves for winter.

A single pair of geese glides in and settles upon the water, no doubt to rest for the night. The light is about gone. The sun has topped a small hill just west of me. It slips down quickly.

Last week I came down to this spot by the river after dark with a flashlight to look for something I had dropped in the tall grass, much of which is bent over and matted down by this time. It was a remarkable experience being down in the grass with a small light and the darkness closed in all around you. It somehow made the bent-over grass stand out like a world unto itself, unlike the way it would appear to us when we tramp over it in broad daylight.

I became aware of the myriad of small channels tunneled under the bent grass, cozy passageways for mice, voles and such. The coming snow would cover it and insulate to 32 degrees or a bit better, providing shelter, food, safety and rest for a world of small creatures.

I return home for a good night's rest. You get a good night's rest, too.

****

Suddenly on the eastern rim of the earth, a tiny crescent of blood red appeared — so red, I did a double-take before I realized it was the rising sun. 8:10 a.m. It grew into the giant orb until it became too bright for the eyes.

A red-tailed hawk swung in over a nearby road, so close that I feared it would collide with the windshield of a passing vehicle. But at the last minute, he deftly veered into the wind and lifted himself safely out of danger. His red tail showed clearly in the morning sun. He drifted off, hunting, I expect, for his breakfast. Perhaps some creature had scooted near the road and led him into danger.

One of the buteo hawks on the prairie we used to call the chicken hawk or hen hawk because, as I understand it, they were accused of preying on free-range hens in poultry yards. I remember hearing, in their defense, that they rarely were known to actually take a chicken. They were rather the farmer's friend for all the field rodents they took. However, like a bad penny, the name kept coming back to attach itself to them.

At the time I was plagued with trying to keep straight whether it was the red-shouldered hawk or the red-tailed hawk that was the chicken hawk. The intervals between seeing them were so long that I couldn't remember.

So I tried a little mnemonics and associated the "sh" of the shoulder with the "ch" of chicken and figured I had aced it. But of course, I was completely wrong. So now I seem to remember it just from recalling that bad memory-try. I've since learned that the red-shouldered hawk is rarely seen in the upper states this far west.

The downy woodpecker hammers on the big elm near me, so he's very much around to entertain me, as is the ever-present chickadee and white-breasted nuthatch. They are all regular visitors at our bird feeders.

As I'm listening to the downy behind me, I notice something unusual about the riverfront before me that I hadn't seen when I sat down among the intermediate wheat grass and tobacco weeds. I normally sit perhaps 40 feet from the river bank. A rough dirt trail runs along the river between me and the bank. Joggers have sometimes passed by along this trail without even noticing me. I've just noticed the trail is now filled with water. Recent heavy rains south of here have overflowed the river to within 12 feet of me.

The river will retreat in a friendly way, leaving the dirt path dry along the river and only a slight dampness in the black loam along the bank. Perhaps it will settle into place for the winter then.

We humans complain about the intrusions the river makes upon our lives, but in point of fact, it is humans who have invaded the natural flood reservoir between the Red and Sheyenne rivers by deciding to settle here. The river, a part of the life force that provides us with the water necessary for our living here, is only doing its natural thing by occasionally overflowing its banks.

Speaking of intrusions, a big red Irish setter challenged me as I was settling down near some tall wood aster stalks. But he only did so in a friendly sort of way, because he came suddenly upon this human animal sitting where the dog was exploring. His master quickly called him off, and he departed for other adventures.

I depart for other adventures, too.

****

I return to the river later in the day. In the waning light of daylight-saving evening, the high brown stalks around me begin to disappear. But remarkably, the small white feather balls of the aster seeds (the little clusters are no more than three-quarter of an inch in diameter) seem to glow in the dusk as if they had a radiance of their own.

As the evening comes on, I can feel a mid-autumn chill settle in around me. It is as if to say, "Your warmth is an intrusion upon my space, here among the grasses tonight."

I remember as a child growing up in Morris, Minn., that we had a prairie area behind our home that we called "the back 40." It was a most wonderful space for a child to have. I recall on a day with a brisk cold wind chilling me on the back 40, I could lie down among the tall grass and feel remarkably warm. It was like a secret that only I knew about.

Geese! Perhaps a few dozen of them fly over me as I am pulled back into the present by the riverside again. They mark their passing with honking. But cloud cover is such that I can only indistinctly make them out with binoculars. I had hoped they might take advantage of the waterway to rest, but they must be warned by snow to the north to keep moving. The sound of their passing disappears in the distance to the south.

Honking and making a general commotion, another flock of perhaps 120 fly over and head south in a very ragged V-formation.

A few moments later, a group of perhaps 40 in smart formation, joined by another 30, fly over, headed north, perhaps to scout out a good resting place for the night. They are certainly on the move on this flyway this week.

By mid-November, most of the migrating birds for this area will have moved through; that is, those that are passers-by. Some migrate this far south and treat us to their company for the winter, like the shrike and snow bunting. Some stay here all year, like the goldfinch, blue jay, horned lark, chickadee and nuthatch.

Bon voyage, my friends. We earthbound creatures remain fixed, while you amazing migratory denizens of the air travel far and wide. We will look forward to your return one day, which will announce to us that spring has come back to the north.

****

Ah, the slate-colored juncos are visiting us now. They add a touch of activity to an otherwise quiet landscape.

As I sit down to view the far bank of the Red River about 70 yards in front of me, it appears at first as if the woods are devoid of animal life. Then I detect a stirring among the leaves near the shore. On training my glasses on the spot, I think at first some fallen ash leaves are blowing about. Then I spot a couple of juncos; and soon they multiply into a dozen, searching the ground for possible seeds.

I have heard that they have come to the area the last few days. Folks see them on their back lawns. Grant's "Common Birds" record them coming through the end of September, though that may be for states further east. However our very warm autumn may have delayed their arrival until now, at the end of October. Their sporty capers among the dry leaves of fall are always a welcome sight.

They will stay here through the winter, and hundreds of them, often being seen by roadsides, will be recorded in our local Christmas bird count (Audubon's longest-running, nationwide bird count conducted by citizens). But in severe weather and compelled by hunger, they will lose their timidity and become quite fearless in coming among us.

Birders say that the junco's note is not much more than a high-pitched trill and is not often heard. Perhaps it is the thin whistle I often hear in the deep grasses in this season but cannot spot the bird itself.

Very likely the junco is most voluble in his mating season in his northern nesting places, far north of here. The experts tell us that only in spring, just upon the eve of his departure, do we hear his song, and we may reasonably suppose he is just tuning up, so to say, for his real nuptial chant. He has a call, while he is still with us, that one ornithologist, Dr. Coues, terms "his snapping note."

Suddenly the woods around me become alive with birds. I hear the familiar chitter of the hairy woodpecker in the giant American elm to my left. The hairy can't seem to eat without commenting as he does so. The elm is completely bare of leaves now, so I can easily spot him as he dances along the big limbs.

Then, all at once, the chickadee calls. I answer it and, turning slowly, I spot him not five feet in front and a little to my right, balancing on some stiff stalks of brome grass looking for edibles. He answers me a few times, and then flies away.

I search for my juncos again across the river, but they seem to have flown, leaving only the dancing, wind-tossed leaves. One leaf settles down onto the river and sails lazily north, out of sight.

****

Settled in today by the Buffalo River east of Glyndon, Minnesota, I'm entertained by the chortle of the shallow stream over rocks and the soft soughing of the wind in the woods.

The river, only eight or nine yards wide at this point, is nevertheless a very active part of the natural surroundings in this region, topping its banks and flooding the area widely in the springtime.

I've wondered why an apparently small river could do so much flooding of such a large area. I've discovered that the river travels only about 200 miles from its source until it empties into the Red River. In that course it drops seven feet per mile, passing along 150 cubic feet of water per second. Add spring rains, winter snows and very flat land, and you have a flood.

At Home in the Woodlands

This is the land of the marbled godwit, the prairie chicken, the upland sandpiper, many deer and the occasional moose. None of those afford me the pleasure of seeing them today, and the woods here by the river are quiet of fauna.

The spot where I am sitting is dry and pleasant, covered with a carpet of brown autumn leaves, after a long period of dryness these last few months. In the spring, this spot would be over my head in flood waters.

I am surrounded by five trees: the green ash, burr oak, cottonwood, basswood and American elm. Except for an odd leaf here and there, all that one has is the bark by which to identify them at this time of year.

I've sometimes wondered how the small creatures manage under the snow during the long winter months, since I did not think that many store up food like the squirrel, whose name we have borrowed as humans, when we "squirrel away" goods for later use. Ordeals of long winters must be a trial for them.

Or do the small creatures store away more food than we realize? I recall having a beanbag exposed one winter, and in the spring at Ham Lake, I found the bean bag empty. Later I discovered the cache of beans neatly stored in the corner of a drawer a long ways away. The creature, likely a mouse, could hardly have carried more than one or two beans at a time to store them.

The basswood, which is also a great favorite of my son and mine for woodcarving, is a great help for these small creatures in the woods, I discovered. In the spring the basswood provides fragrant blossoms that attract innumerable insects. In the autumn, they cover the forest floor with winged seeds that offer an abundant harvest for mice. So I expect that, whether or not these mice store food, the forest floor beneath the blanket of snow is covered with enough food to sustain them through the winter.

The little lively stream continues its babbling as the evening settles in. It will only be silenced for a time when winter covers it with a cloak of ice and adorns it with winter silence.

****

A gentle morning breeze caresses the land. The tall white asters and tobacco weed dance gracefully in the wind.

A small hawk takes off suddenly from the giant willow tree to my left and flies across the river and into the trees too quickly for me to identify him. Where had he been perched? He surprised me. I'd been observing the trees around me for half an hour and had not seen him. Perhaps some crows will arrive and badger him into action again.

The white asters, on the other hand, are at their glorious best. A lovely cluster weaves about in the breeze about 10 inches from my right shoulder at eye level as I sit here. They have an exquisite little white flower about three-quarters of an inch across with a deep gold center. Each petal is a narrow white blade a quarter inch long, and I count 36 petals radiating out from the golden center. The brown remnants of these little blossoms have remained with me far into the fall when I come down here, as a quiet reminder of their former beauty. They were here yet this spring. Where are these brown husks now? Do they just quietly lie down and disappear and give way to the new generation?

At Home in the Woodlands

The giant ragweed towers about, some of it up to four feet in height. My Iowa mentor, David Osheim, has helped me identify it, for I had inquired about a month or so ago. The ragweed was headed out at that time, each branch boasting four or five bold, brown heads, but these heads have mostly shed their seeds now. The giant ragweed, or horseweed, as it is sometimes called, has a three-lobed leaf and a burred stem that is rough to the touch. Under ideal conditions, it can reach heights of 12 feet. It bears a green blossom that is always only green. It must bear some kind of fragrance, though, for I see small bees are attracted to it.

The tobacco weed is at its tobacco-looking best now, with dark brown stalks and clusters that very much stand out among the greenery around it. I can't remember catching sight of it to notice it when it was young. Was it green then? It turns tobacco-brown very early.

The riparian area has taken on a remarkable verdure this year, perhaps largely due to the fact that it was completely spared of being scraped down to the mud flat by flood and ice this spring. The abundance of plant species is wonderful.

The crows have set up a ruckus across the river. They must have discovered the predator. He likely left quietly, for they've now quieted down themselves.

The chickadee greets me as well, flitting among the branches of the big willow tree to my left. He notifies me of his presence with his light che-che call even before I spot him. Of course, he will be a constant visitor and companion throughout the winter months here in the north.

These are warm autumn days, and the house fly and several small white butterflies sport about among the tall grass in the morning sun. A small bee with yellow and black markings lights on my jacket and warms himself in the sun. He means me no harm and presently zips away to a nearby thistle that strikes his fancy.

The little ash tree directly in front of me intrigues me. It is entirely new growth this spring. It has stopped its upward growth at four feet but has put out a healthy set of leaves, which are starting to turn yellow now. I assume it spent some time putting down stout roots. It has a trunk of less than one inch in diameter.

No other small tree has survived the floods and spring ice in this open area for 40 feet or so in any direction. But this last unusual spring, with no floods or overflowing ice, enabled new plants like this ash tree to set down roots an get a good start. I have noticed that if tree seedlings take root in your garden, you need to pull them out quickly because, within weeks, they set in roots that make them impossible to pull out by hand. So will this young white ash be a survivor? Next spring we will see.

A male indigo bunting wings silently across my line of vision and deftly perches on one of the four-foot stalks of thistles, 15 feet in front of me. He stays long enough for me to get my glasses on him and study him.

My first impression is the blue of his coloring. It is not the deep blue of summer, for he has taken on his faded fall coloring, but the blue still catches my attention, as does the dark crest on his head.

A few minutes later the female indigo lands on a willow branch. She bears the sparrow-like appearance but without any of the distinctive streaks or wing bars of any of the sparrows. The two busy themselves seed hunting among the tall weeds.

A belted kingfisher flies in front of me above the river, propelled by his erratic wing beat, announcing himself with his rattling voice. A moment after, another kingfisher follows him, and they disappear into the white oaks to my left.

The tall weeds and trees are fairly alive with birds this afternoon, unlike lazy midsummer afternoons that are almost devoid of bird life. We are enjoying the migration of birds through our northern states. The yellow warblers and hummingbirds have left to begin their travels south. We can put away our hummingbird feeders now and welcome back the friendly little hummers when they return in the spring.

We interrupt this program to announce that a warbler, with his gray hood and bright, bright yellow lower breast, is promenading through the tall weeds in front of me. He gives me a good chance to look at him. Now he moves off to my right and disappears into the tall grass.

The Blackburnian and Magnolia Warblers, which I am not seeing today, are also migrating through at this time. This is a wonderful time for twitchers, as the British call birdwatchers, to be out warbler-watching. Your local Audubon Club, if it is active, will be organizing such early morning bird hikes, if you've a bit of the twitcher in you.

Last week several men from the Audubon Club took us on an early morning birding excursion to see the warblers and other birds in migration through this area. These trips are always helpful to me, because these fellows are so much better and quicker at identification than I and thus give me a chance to see more birds. I had the joy of adding three birds to my life list: the great crested flycatcher, the Blackburnian warbler and the red-eyed vireo. This is a wonderful birding season.

An interesting development is that the Canada thistle in front of me has put out a new blossom, one of its lovely deep purple blooms, since last week. Almost every thistle nearby has dried its blossoms and put out the white cotton ball it makes when it sheds seeds. I assumed they were done for the season, especially since we had a sharp frost last night. Now I see new flower buds on some stalks.

The moon has just risen over a young oak across the river. He is early in his rising, as it is only late afternoon, but the moon has his own agenda. He heralds the coming evening.

Now six more small birds are peopling the tall weeds in front of me. With some excitement I am grabbing my glasses to see what I can discover. So if you will excuse me, this is me, signing off, from twitcher heaven.

****

A song sparrow flies into the branches of an old stunted prairie willow near the river bank 15 feet from me. He flits about among the branches, giving me a good chance to see the black spot on his streaked breast and the rufous crown on his head.

As autumn proceeds we see the house wren and brown thrasher leave for warmer climes. The white-throated sparrow appears, and then passes through all too quickly, sporting about on the ground while he is here, going after whatever seeds he can find. Or else you'll discover him under the feeders, picking at whatever mess nuthatches or chickadees carelessly scatter off the feeder.

Appearing now in their migration and staying a little longer are the golden-crowned kinglet and the pine siskin. The old birders of a century ago, like John Grant, called the latter a pine finch; and, indeed, he is a finch.

Many of the siskins will remain with us over the winter. The Christmas bird count recently recorded over 50 for this area. But no kinglets did they record, so they will leave soon to fly south.

A downy woodpecker sails into the young white oak in front of me, checks it out and then travels on. He, of course, is a welcome saucy winter resident with us in this area. Perhaps he will return to visit me today before I leave. The young oak has a wood duck house on it.

A group of eastern kingbirds fly into the very top branches, now bare of leaves, of the tall oak to the left. The white band on the ends of their tails is evident. The kingbirds dash off the ends of their perches from time to time, and return to perch again. I expect they are going after insects, as they are flycatchers. They always impress me as sitting rather proudly, as if their perches were thrones and they were kings indeed.

Where I sit, the area round me for about 30 square feet is covered with large plantain leaves which are still green after several frosts. The area circling them is covered with tall plants four and five feet high. But in the enclosed area, the plantain seems to be curiously dominant and only here and there does a taller plant struggle up among them and stand tall in their midst. The plantain lies flat on the ground, like a mat on the forest floor.

My neighbors around me, as I sit here, are those plants with the rich, brown color that I've referred to many times. I have cavalierly called them tobacco weed, for they aptly fit the description. However for this plant, I must correct the record. I took a specimen down to David Osheim last week, and he identified it immediately as sourdock. So there you have it. But some of you may have referred to it by that common name yourselves, for "tobacco weed" is not original with me. The name, indeed, fits the plant.

The oaks and ashes are mostly bare now. The giant willow to my right still keeps its leaves, though. A downy works on a big white oak behind me. He is always busy after that morsel under the bark.

A flock of agitated crows are badgering a predator across the river. I can see the villain trying to elude them but he is too far away for me to identify. It may be an owl. Perhaps they will chase him over to this side before I finish so I can get a good look.

The tall brome grass that reaches up around me as I sit here is half brown and half green yet, after some sharp frosts at night over the past months. Their slender green leaves are tough and handle frost well.

This area is experiencing drought now, but the flora looks amazingly good. The river is low as it has been in quite some time. In places near here, it is only three feet deep. Experts tell us that prairie grasses have a tremendous ability to cope with drought. They develop roots that run four to 10-feet deep and sometimes deeper, searching for water.

If the drought is too severe and long-lasting, these grasses are even capable of going into repose and awaiting the return of rain. My wife recalls the grasses around her home in Mott, in western North Dakota, looking entirely brown and dead in the late 1930s, yet coming alive again after some rain. I wonder if they develop an ability to live off resources of the living roots, even, as they say, the human body can live off its body resources for a time during periods of starvation.

These sturdy prairie grasses are those such as the big bluestem (nicknamed turkey foot for the shape of their leaf clusters) and the little bluestem. As I recall, the brome grass is not one of them but is one that invaded our area (to very useful and beneficial effect) after the plowing up of native prairie sod. If the drought is severe and long enough, it will disappear.

A nuthatch prances up and down the overhanging bare branches of the big American elm above me, just 20 feet away, hunting for food tidbits. He announces his presence with his silly uck-uck note, as if he cannot peck the branches without making noise at the same time.

A single crow wings its way lazily across the river in front of me and disappears beyond the treeline on the other side. A fellow crow sounds off casually to my left. I am sure they will return to entertain me again before I leave.

Aha! Just when I think there is no other life astir about me on this autumn day, I see a tiny tan-white spider climbing up his web to the twig of a white ash that hangs down in front of me. He is so small I think at first he is only a speck of dust. But then I see him progress steadily up his invisible web and clamber onto the twig. What has brought him out into this near-freezing air?

And now an unusual visitor arrives; a small predator. He remains a long time and gives me a good chance to study him through the glasses, although he is at some distance. But I am able to study both his appearance and antics.

He appears to be a kestrel, a sparrow hawk. He looks back and forth, from left to right. Occasionally he spreads his wings a bit, and then settles back to watch. He does not evince the flightiness of most small birds but rather sits boldly in command of the moment, very much the hunter. Then suddenly he dives down and disappears into the lower trees. He has been sitting atop an almost-dead tall ash. What did he discover and go after?

A flock of geese passes overhead, too high for me to see them above the overcast. But I can hear their calling. We are now passing through the final phase of the migration through our area. The busy activity of our lively migrants comes to an end.

The robins will go, along with the meadowlarks, grackles, red-winged blackbirds and vesper sparrows. Our winter visitors will move in from the north to join us like the snow bunting and the shrike. Of course we'll always enjoy our permanent residents like the chickadees and the nuthatches at our feeders.

I'm sure someone will say to me, "But I have seen a robin at Christmas." And I must admit that is true. A few stout-hearted robins, who find enough here to eat, are discovered here at every Christmas bird count.

At Home in the Woodlands

Yet our red-breasted friend will always remain our favorite herald of spring. Then he will entertain us with pulling worms out of the ground.

I remember as a child growing up in central Minnesota, I could always depend on seeing my first robin by the first of April. Yet, strange as it may seem, I could see them arrive on the first of April in the Yukon, when we lived there in later years. They seemed to have no sense of geography.

I notice that the giant willow near the river bank still retains its leaves this far into the fall. All the others have shed them by now.

Is it the narrower leaves on the willow that enables them to escape the frost and retain leaves this long? The narrow leaves or blades of the brome grass near me are still green in like manner.

A few turkeys roamed off to my right and completely disappeared for a while. Now they are back again in force, directly across the river from me. Perhaps they disappeared into the dense brush to my right. I can hear their kuk-kuk sound. They, at least, are enjoying these late autumn days.

The white aster greets me today, to the right of where I sit. It always offers welcome autumn companionship late into the fall, even surviving the first frosts.

It boasts a small exquisite blossom, the size of a nickel, with 36 white narrow petals and a yellow center. At the moment it seems to be the only flower in this riverside area.

I do see bright yellow coloring on a 2-foot plant some distance to my right. But at closer examination, I see it is the lovely golden-yellow of a plant that has turned color early, and it glows in the autumn sun. It stands out, because this riparian area is almost entirely green yet, from good rains.

This autumn day, with the leaves partly fallen, gives me a last chance to identify the trees in this place along the river before winter comes and I have only a bare stand of forest surrounding me. A surprising number are green ash, but the basswood, with its smoother bark, is sprinkled among them. The oaks and maples are more scarce here, but they must be here enough to attract the gray squirrels. The rain continues gently, its patter the only sound now on this quiet morning.

Except for a little activity and the soft patter of the rain, the woods seem quiet. I am made aware that to let the quiet of the woods seep into me, I must set aside for a few moments, the customary chatter of human activity: radios, cell phones and talking. The quiet of the woods stands aside and waits for this clatter to subside before it approaches one. Then it quietly nestles about a person and just rests there.

Although the day in the woods is mostly gray, it is alive with the reddish color of reed canary grass. I have seen this plant on other sites on the river but never in such abundance. It rises tall and lush and is beautiful in its autumn red-brown color on dried stalks. It would be the delight of an artist who might like to capture this autumn scene.

Its branches are spotted with hundreds of tiny seed pods that give it the appearance of knotted rope. Each seed pod breaks open to dozens of tiny seeds, which means each plant produces thousands of such seeds. Nature is profligate.

When I pluck the stem of an identical plant next to it, I notice that the broken end of the stem emits a sticky milky substance onto my fingers. Is it a kind of milkweed? I shall have to get help identifying it.

I am curious to know why this plant has turned a showy golden color while all of its cousins still wear their rich summer green. Then I see that a small grape vine has grown up the length of this golden plant, tightly gripping it with its tentacles, and has apparently strangled it. Its bright golden flag is like a signal for help that has come too late.

I am impressed with how there is change amidst no change in the same area that I return to again and again. Certainly there is change from year to year, which I have mentioned, but the same area offers changes from week to week. I expect that if I looked closely, I could see change from day to day. If I were an extremely keen observer, which I am not, I'm sure I could see change from moment to moment.

Of course that change in a moment is true, because now as I see a single golden leaf flutter to the ground from high in a green ash tree, I am seeing change. The tree has changed, and the ground where the leaf landed has changed.

There is a certain sense in which nature offers me moment-to-moment snapshots that it behooves me to drink in and enjoy, for they will never be repeated in history. Perhaps that is why we humans are admonished to "stop and smell the roses," as they say.

A few old friends seem constant. The giant 60-foot prairie willow to my left, with its 24-foot circumference, is faithfully here whenever I return, it seems. The 80-foot giant American elm, with its 10-foot base, under which I sit, will always be here, it seems, to shelter me from the beating of the summer sun.

Yet I know that if I were to live another century and come back, even these old friends would be gone. And one day, I am gone, too, and someone else comes down to this river to fish or read or paint or write.

****

A flock of chipping sparrows greets me on the far side of the Red River this afternoon. They frolic about among the tall grasses, and a few of them perch atop a small log in the waning sun and give a good chance to study them through my glasses.

Their banding together surprises me a little, as I usually see them singly on the ground, hunting for food. Is this perhaps a part of the flocking together I hear so much about among birds of a kind as they prepare for the migration south? It is interesting how these groups spend some days together before they begin the journey.

Earlier this fall in Glacial Lake State Park in Minnesota, I saw a flock of perhaps 50 starlings careening about in a wonderful aerial exhibition. A week ago I viewed several hundred doves lined up on a wire alongside a road. What secret communication brings these birds together at this time of year?

A blue jay just called from a tall ash tree at the river's edge. I whistled back, but he decided I didn't look like a jay and flew off.

The long brome grass is still lush and green all about, but it is beginning to bend over everywhere, nodding its tips to the ground. The central body of the plants still rises up, so the whole effect is that of undulating waves of green, flowing out away from me.

Similar waves of brown stalks (last year's growth perhaps) appear among the green billows. These brown waves are stiff and hard from the drying of the stalks, and they are matted together in a firm network. It occurs to me that these little canopies will hold up as snow falls on them, and they will provide excellent havens for small creatures through the dead of winter.

The insect world seems to have mostly left this area by this time of year. However a small brown moth, no bigger than a flax seed, flutters past slowly and heads for some tall grass. A moment later a small black insect lands on the knuckle of my index finger and begins to explore. He is no larger than a quarter inch of pencil lead. He seems undisturbed by my movements and prances about on my finger as if he owned the place.

Who are these late-leavers of the insect world? It is time to tell them that soon they, too, must retire for the long winter's sleep.

****

We love to find some excuse to return to Ham Lake in the late fall. Perhaps it is to take in a dock we have purposely left in the lake for that excuse. Perhaps it is just to see the late, fading autumn as it makes its last sigh before giving way to winter.

A chickadee darts into the stand of poplars where I sit near the lake, my first visitor since I have settled down and quit making any disturbance. He checks out the bark of a poplar tree and then moves on.

Although the temperature in the area today is quite chilly and even freezing at night, nestled in this poplar stand in the deep woods under a morning sun and a cloudless sky, I am almost too warm in the layers of clothing I am wearing. I can well imagine how deer and other woodland creatures would find a welcome place of refuge here under such a sun

One sees poplars about in all directions, as far as the eye can see. They are all young, none more than 20 feet tall nor two inches in diameter. I am facing due south. The sun, although only at about 45 degrees, is at its highest point for the day, which makes it near noon. If I would lift the visor of my cap, I would stare directly into the sun.

One of the delights of facing sunward is that the sun discloses the array of spider webs in a stand of close woods like this. The sun makes them shimmer in the slight zephyr of a breeze as we have today. To my surprise, the webs boast different colors, beautiful colors — a deep gold on one, an iridescent blue on another.

I conclude that the different colors are due to different compositions in the webs. The movement of the sun informs me, I am soon to discover, that my conclusion is completely wrong. As the sun moves, the colors on the webs transform themselves. The gold one becomes blue and the blue, gold.

Summer seems to ease into a rest toward its end, making its chlorophyll, warming its limbs and branches and soils. A few insects have begun weaving their cocoons. But all in all, it seems the summer season has become a time for sitting comfortably in the shade, or basking in the warm summer sun.

Then, suddenly, it is as if an alarm clock has gone off, and all things are hastening to jump into their shirts and trousers and rush off to the day's work. There is matter to be laid down to begin decomposing for next year's soil. There are warm nests to be made and acorns to be stored against the winter cold.

A small butterfly of the cabbage butterfly type, but more yellow, flits amiably by where I sit. He surprises me, as I thought such insects would be gone by now. He lands on one tiny sapling, then flies to another, on and on, until he is out of sight. Apparently he is seeking food. He is still around to soak up the warm morning October sun. He passes too quickly for me to identify him.

The other day a beautiful mourning cloak butterfly visited my backyard — a lovely creature with his black cloak fringed in white, and the distinctive markings on his upper wings. He traveled into the house accidentally on a basket of laundry, so I had an excellent opportunity to observe him. I finally slipped a sheet of paper under his feet and carried him out of doors in the evening. He was gone by morning. Such visits are real gems for the observer.

The insect life is amazingly active in this warm spot on a cold autumn day — a small version of a house fly, a tiny gnat with transparent wings, and a large ant, half red and half black. The latter is busy, for a moment later I spy him traveling across the rim of the visor of my cap.

While this stand of trees consists mostly of poplars, it includes a smattering of other trees. I see a lovely little paper birch in front of me, no more than an inch in diameter. About 15 feet in front of me I see a red oak, still sporting its reddish brown fall colors, while all of the poplars and birches are bare.

To the left I see a small white oak, about an inch in diameter. And in the distance I can see a few Norway pines towering above the poplar stand. For the moment, the poplars dominate the oaks. In time, of course, all that will change and the oaks will rise slowly and establish themselves as dominant.

I've paused for a moment now, sitting on a log. Lady, our lab, sits a few feet away, looking directly at me as if to say, "This is no way to carry on a decent romp." Then she quickly finds other mysteries to explore in the woods about us.

A gray squirrel suddenly breaks out chattering nearby, startling me. He's been gathering acorns, for I see a few on the log in front of his tree. I think he has just discovered Lady and me. He sits on a low branch of a maple, scolding us, perhaps saying, "Please go away now and don't disturb me anymore."

The sun shines into this little break in the woods where I sit. It feels mighty good, because the air is chilly. Directly ahead, a flaming red maple flashes its brilliance at me. The leaves are like colored windows with the sun shining through them. A slight breeze moves them, shimmering, and their crimson seems to dance and ripple through the branches. Second only to the sumac nearby, the red maple boasts the fanciest display, one surrounded by a golden sea of birches and cottonwoods.

And now to complete the picture, against the deep, deep blue patch of sky beyond the maple, a great cotton ball of cumulus cloud hovers into view, making its way across the patch of blue behind the flaming red. That ball of brightest white moves rather quickly, suggesting a much swifter movement of the air up high than what I'm feeling here below.

A redstart near me! He is late. He must wish to add to the fall colors.

And now Lady reminds me with a noisy yawn that it's time to move on. She's had enough of exploring this spot.

So I stand and stretch the laziness out of my limbs. I can feel the sun through my wool shirt. It seems like the warmth of it reflects from all the color around me. I feel contented.

Now I start down into the woods and across country with Lady beside me. We skirt a small pond, spangled with leaves of gold and red floating on it, and head across the point.

If the redstart still watches, the woods now close behind me.

Finally the season of autumn must wind down, and we must prepare for the coming winter at Ham Lake. We drain the water pipes and bring in the dock. It is with a kind of a sigh that we shut down another summer-autumn season. But we vaguely realize that without the shutting down, we would not have the glorious "opening up" in the spring.

The river carries a flotilla of ash seeds on its surface today, bearing them north downstream to some unknown destination that will catch and hold them, ready for spring sprouting. From where I stand on the river's edge I can see many such rafts of seeds, some of them caught and held among the tree roots already along the bank. Among these collections, I spot a small smattering of elm seeds joining the migration.

Burrs of various kinds catch themselves on my trousers and socks hitching a ride with me, their way of traveling and spreading their seeds. It is the season of sowing seeds for wild plants to prolong their species.

One matter that strikes me as interesting is the lack of waterfowl on this stretch of the Red River in the last two years; none, that I can recall. I miss them a great deal.

Before that time, Canada geese and ducks of all kinds entertained me every week during the mating and the migrating seasons. They gave me great aerial shows, dashing across my line of vision just above the surface of the river. The drakes made a great show of competing for mates and finally coupled up.

Sometimes they would fly a few rods upstream and then lazily ride the gentle current back down to me. Or perhaps they would climb up on the bank and sun themselves awhile.

I am left wondering the reason for the absence of waterfowl at this particular pace. One does not want to draw hasty conclusions but perhaps after two years, I might be forgiven for making a few surmises.

At Home in the Woodlands

The last two years here on the river have been drier than the previous decade. Two years ago the river did not even rise over its banks in the spring, which was quite remarkable. Last year it only came up a little and then receded. I pondered whether in drier seasons, waterfowl seek wetter flyways? The Red River here has kept its 55-yard stretch of water from bank to bank, which makes it seem the same to us; but perhaps not to waterfowl.

A late season robin sounds his low trill from a nearby white oak tree, as if to reassure me that I am not entirely bereft of bird life. He is not moving, though; perhaps settling down for the evening.

A gray squirrel lopes amiably across an open space to my left and then up an oak tree. Squirrels are smiling here this year. This season has seen a bumper crop of acorns. We have raked up whole tubs filled with them. Perhaps that is why he is so amiable. I am sure he has his winter den well stocked with enough acorns to see him through a long winter if needs be.

Power to you, my friend!

****

A week later the scene has changed. A red squirrel has hopped across a small opening 10 yards in front of me and climbed a small ash tree. He moved quite casually, as if not bothered by me. A very light snow here, our first, has made his tracks quite good. I can see plainly the four small prints in a cluster; the two front ones spread apart a little, the back ones together, as if to gather strength for springing.

The tiny claws in each print are quite plain, two in front and one on each side. The whole print of his paw is no larger than my thumbprint, which I put beside it in the snow. He jumps about 40 inches on each bound, so he is in no great hurry. How amazing that he can grab a tree or even a stucco wall and climb up it.

The woods begin to look more like winter now, with the dusting of snow. The brown of the forest floor leaf covering is now festooned with white. Creatures cannot go by now without leaving traces of their passing. In summer they could be more secretive.

A flock of 50 crows circles silently above me as I sit by the river and then drifts away to the west, as if going nowhere in particular. Why their sudden appearance in a sky that had been devoid of birds for the past hour?

In a few minutes the answer appears above the trees from the east across the river. A Cooper's hawk comes into view, headed my way. I pick him up in my binoculars and study him for a good while as he circles back and forth casually above me, playing with the air drafts and the gusts of autumn wind. He circles in this fashion for a while and then drifts to the west, out of sight.

Thrushes, sparrows, wrens and warblers will leave for warmer climes by this week or so. However the ground sparrows (white-throated and white crowned), the kinglets and pine finches are yet to come through. Some other summer birds like the ovenbird, song sparrow, flickers and purple finches, will still be with us for a few weeks more.

The big elm above has lost all of its leaves, and its branches are spidery fingers silhouetted against the last vestiges of the dying light in the evening sky. The first stars appear in the darkened heavens, and the planet Venus is the brightest among them at the moment.

The crows have not returned, so old Cooper must still be shuttling them on west.

Time for hawks and crows to come to roost, too.

*****

Autumn has been vivid in bringing constant change all about. Week by week, colors have changed. Moment by moment, occasional brisk breezes have picked up brown leaves and danced them about as if on parade.

Now pace of change picks up as the season rushes on toward winter, and we may as well acknowledge that autumn has come to a close, as well. And one day, the first flecks of white snow will fall gently to earth to rest upon all that was autumn.

Mowers and combines we put away in machine sheds, taking time only to lubricate and tend to them to prepare them for the next coming phase of spring and winter. We pack away our shorts and sandals, and take out our boots and long johns. We put away our golf clubs and tennis rackets and polish up our skis and skates, considering with as much relish the joys of this winter phase as we did the pleasures of summer. It is time once again for the winter phase of our cycles of seasons.

The snow will come and go for a week or two, suggesting a lingering wish for autumn to remain a little longer. But the die is cast. Winter approaches to lay his claim to the land. The glories of autumn must retire gracefully for another year. It is the end of the season of yellows and reds and brilliant golds.

Chapter 3: Snow and Fresh Footprints

As autumn disappears into winter, there's an extra briskness in the air, and one dons a warm jacket regularly now, whenever going outside. This transition into cooler weather comes at the time of the American "Thanksgiving" holiday, as if the pilgrim fathers knew it was time to bring to a close another growing season, to give thanks to God for blessing them with a bountiful harvest, and to prepare for the rigors of a coming winter.

Winter charges in as a crisis time for any of us. It raises the question, "What will we do with the coming months?"

"Avoid it," some answer, and go south for the winter.

Others answer, "Pretend it is not here." They may go out of heated homes, into heated garages and preheated cars, drive into a heated garage at work, and go up into heated offices.

I once did a tally and found that more people die in November than in any other month of the year. And the second highest month is March. November and March — the bookends of winter. I guess dying would be another way of getting out of winter.

But I'm not going to run away. I'm not going to hide.

I find winter is a time to pause. Stand still. Silently. Let the freshness of blessing wash over me like a cool breeze at the end of a hot day. It is perhaps in these acknowledgements of the rhythms of life that we humans really get in touch with that Earth on which our feet are planted. And it is perhaps for this getting in touch with the Earth that humans will most be remembered when our time, like that of the dinosaurs, is past.

A gray squirrel clings upside down to the trunk of an oak tree and chatters, as if to say, "Others may have gone underground and out of sight for the season, but I want you to know that I am still around and going about my business." And with that he scampers up an ash tree and out of sight.

He has left his prints clearly on the thin covering of snow, showing his four toes and the small "thumb" at the side of his foot. The tracks suggest he has ambled casually across the forest floor, without fear or excitement, and then tracks disappear near the base of the tree where, sporty and agile, he has taken a sizeable leap from his last tracks to the tree trunk.

The upside of winter over summer in the forest, with winter's light overnight snowfalls, is the opportunity to discover fresh tracks in the snow in the morning, which one rarely sees in the summer, unless it's along a sandy beach.

At Home in the Woodlands

In the winter, whatever has gone by your favorite woodland spot before has passed again that morning to treat you to a fresh delight. No matter who you are, you always find that fresh tracks are fun. For a moment, when you stop to observe them, you have become a tracker.

Now I am talking about the novice, not the expert tracker, like those in Steinbeck's "The Pearl," who can discover meaning in a bent twig. I'm talking about those who are finding delight in their first tracks.

First you discover these tracks, and those tracks, and those other tracks. You don't know to whom they belong, but judging from the traffic in the neighborhood, they belong to squirrels, rabbits and deer.

After you've sorted out whose is whose, you scratch your head and ask yourself, which direction were they going? Do they make the trail in the snow by their tracks as they are landing or as they are taking off on the next leap? Since we don't have an expert around to answer that, we have to observe the animal in action, bounding over the fresh snow, and then go and observe the tracks and trail markings. Then you become an expert.

Direction offers some interesting puzzles. With the squirrel, for example, you observe the two tiny prints of the forepaws and then the great big tracks of the hind paws that make him appear to be going east. Then you observe him in action and discover he actually places his hind paws in front of his front paws, much as you do when you are playing leap frog with friends. So instead, that squirrel is going west.

Next you wrinkle your face a bit and ask yourself how fast the animal was going. Was he taking a leisurely stroll through the woods, or was he frightened and heading pell-mell for the nearest safety? You observe the distance between tracks and the flared nature of the individual prints. You draw your conclusion. But remembering your misconceptions upon observing the direction, you wait to see the animal go by to corroborate the evidence.

The forest floor has only a dusting of snow on it yet, but enough to become alive with the tell-tale footprints of creatures that pass across it, part of the wonder of the season of snow in the woods. Before the snow, the passing of these creatures was invisible to us. Now tracks will be interesting to study as the snow increases. Each fresh snow will suggest how recently some animal has passed by.

Tracks identified by four or five claws seem to be the only markings around here. No three-toed sloths in these parts. A dog or cat will show four, as well as a fox, rabbit or mink. A 'coon will show five, as well as an otter and skunk.

The Red River appears to have come to a standstill. It has, of course, only skinned over with ice for the season, stiff enough so that a rock dropped upon it does not penetrate that covering. Meanwhile the heart of the river still pulses under the ice, as it continues its journey north to Lake Winnipeg. The ice is as smooth as glass on the river's surface.

The ice and the water under it are a mystery all by themselves. The water offers itself to us as a life-giving source and then impishly hides under a shell of its own making. Humans and other animals must somehow find their way to it to survive.

At Home in the Woodlands

As winter stretches on, the Red River will seem to become a narrow black stream flowing lazily between stretches of bright, white snow-covered ice that push out more and more from the shore toward the center. One day the stretches will meet and make the river a secret beneath, where it will continue its life flow until the spring thaw. On it goes.

I lived in the Yukon for six years. During that time, I remember visiting a trapper, Don Lange, at his cabin along his trap line in the Yukon. He took a few of us out on the ice of the lake by his cabin, (not far from Robert Service's famous Lake Lebarge) to set fish nets for a catch for supper. I wondered how he would stretch the net in a lake covered with ice. He cut two ice holes about 50 feet apart and remarkably "walked" a primitive wooden device under the ice from one hole to another. We had fish for supper.

During the netting process, I asked Don some questions. I noticed the water overflow around the ice holes, but our good modern boots kept our feet dry. I asked how the Indians with their moccasins managed to keep dry. He told me how they would wet their moccasins, let them freeze to form a coating of ice and after that, they were impervious to water.

Later I asked him if the early Native Canadians, who had no central heating, were able to keep any food that they did not want to freeze when they were away from their dwellings for several days at a time. We take these conveniences for granted.

Don explained that they would put the perishables into a sealed container or sealed bag and push the container through the ice hole and down under the ice. Of course the water around them would never fall below 32 degrees.

I'm often a little skeptical of the possible yarns these woods experts might tell to us dudes. So I tried the preservation later at Ham Lake near Walker. It worked. Some apples and oranges came out as fresh and unfrozen as you please. We humans learn to live with our ice/water environment.

I recall venturing out onto lake ice during winter days on Leech Lake's Templar Point. The ice bridge for winter ran by there, from Onigum to Walker. It always took the DNR's OK and the first brave soul to make the crossing to get traffic started. Then suddenly a 17-mile trip from Onigum to Walker became a one-mile trip in a matter of minutes.

I remember my first crossing in our pickup. I was an absolute coward, even though many people obviously had crossed already. I drove all the way with my front door open, ready to jump out if need be. It all went just fine.

Ice is both ominous and rewarding. That could be said of all of life in the woods in winter, and it is what makes the woods both mysterious and wondrous.

****

In the white expanse of snow in front of me today, it seems as if a giant flamenco dance went on last night in the moonlight. The tracks are all rabbits and squirrels.

The rabbits may well have been out in the moonlight, but the gray squirrels likely made their tracks yesterday in the fresh dusting of snow and were comfortably hunkered down for the night in their nests when all of that night life went on. The cottontails find the nights safer from predators, as they can't scurry up a tree to safety like the squirrel. Squirrels are amazing climbers, dashing up and down trees and across stucco building walls as if vertical surfaces were as easy as horizontal.

As I look at the Red River 100 yards in front of me, now completely covered with ice, I'm reminded of another incident along this same Red River, 70 miles to the north at Grand Forks. My cousin was shooting a gray squirrel high up in a towering ash tree.

I was very young at the time when I stood there watching him, and I was not sure why he was doing this. I grew up concluding this was just something that boys ages 12 to 92 did. I observed they often ate the creatures they shot, but I somehow concluded my cousin was not planning to eat this little fellow.

What I do recall is that my cousin hit the gray seven times before he brought him to the ground. After each hit, the little fellow dropped several feet, but each time he gamely caught hold of a branch and rescued himself. After the seventh hit, he hadn't enough life in him to rescue himself and he fell to the ground. I looked at his limp body lying at my feet and, as a young boy, I must have concluded something. But I can't remember what it was. Perhaps you could tell me.

Now gray squirrels make flamenco dance tracks for me in the snow and delightfully entertain me by this same river, more than half a century later.

****

I arrive to visit another woods on a brisk winter day. Six degrees below zero this morning, I am on the banks high above the Mississippi River.

The Mississippi offers a sharp contrast to the Red River, my usual site for watching and waiting in the woods. The high banks rise perhaps 60 feet above the Mighty Mississippi; for the Red, it's merely a four-foot drop. And the Red's 55-yard span feels like a lazy country stream compared to the perhaps 200-yard spread where I sit on the Mississippi.

I come upon two yearling deer and approach cautiously. They see me, but they do not spook — they gaze at me and amble off leisurely. I follow carefully at a distance and discover two older whitetails bedded down in a copse of small pine trees. They see me, but they don't seem greatly disturbed by my presence, as long as I keep my distance.

I am curious whether they clear the snow first, and then bed down. But I prefer not to disturb them, and I move off. Perhaps I can return and inspect the spot later.

The red oaks and maples range themselves below the lip of the high banks, so that their tops seem almost close enough to touch. A giant cottonwood among them stands like a silent winter sentinel.

Out of the corner of my eye I catch the sight of a red squirrel, bold in the cold, descending the shaggy bark of a big white oak. He pauses in the snow tree and digs a bit. Is he burying something? Or is he digging up something — an acorn or two, perhaps, that he knows he secreted there in the fall? He lopes across the snow in arched leaps, as if he didn't want to get his belly cold from the snow. As he climbs a big maple, I notice he didn't bother to cover up his diggings. Upon examination, I find he seems to have left nothing there except a couple of oak leaves but has dug under the grass just a few inches, so perhaps he has retrieved something.

At Home in the Woodlands

The white flash of what appears to be a small hawk scoots by in front of me perhaps 30 feet away. He flies by at eye level, darting through the trees. He has passed by too quickly to be identified. Is he in a perpetual search for food, perhaps mice under the snow, or perhaps small birds huddled in the low bushes for warmth? The drive for food presses all of us creatures out of our cozy abodes in search of it.

I recall Darwin remarking upon predator and prey, which seems to us like a merciless construction in nature. Yet under that construction, it seems necessary.

Nature provides in seeming profligate measure, the prey. Mice, for example, proliferate exponentially, in a manner that would seem to overrun the planet, if not somehow held in check. Hence, the predator.

To us, the killing seems cruel. But the great naturalist eases our minds by suggesting that death is quick and not lingering (it would seem cats with mice are an exception). And life in its larger sense moves on, as indeed it does this winter day, like Old Man River, down there below these high banks.

Today is Winter Solstice. The shortest day of the year. Tomorrow will be a few minutes longer.

The sun has reached its farthest point south, and now it will begin to move north to warm us Northerners again. There is a kind of hope built into that cycle. Perhaps it is a model for the human, who returns again after he has reached the greatest depths in his fortunes.

Of course we understand that the sun does not move at all, but it is the revolutions of our tilted planet about the sun that creates the effect of this cycle of the coming and going of the sun. However, although we know better by this time in human history, we still like to retain a little of that sense that the Universe revolves around us. Perhaps we can be forgiven this little arrogance.

****

Twenty degrees below zero! Sun dogs greet me around the morning sun over the Red River. They flash bold rainbows in the frosty air on either side of the sun, against a pale blue sky.

What creatures could possibly want to come out in this cold?

And yet I am no sooner settled here by the Red River than 23 wild turkeys come up from the river woods not 60 yards ahead of me. It seems hunger will overcome extreme discomfort. A few bolder ones come closer, both toms and hens, and pass by me, just six or eight feet away. They seem wary, but not intimidated. They never look straight at me with both eyes, as the deer do, but rather look at me with one eye, standing sideways, as if prepared for flight.

A curious bird. Those bare feet and legs must be sinew and cartilage; flesh would freeze. If I were walking unshod and unmittened out on that snow, my fingers and toes would indeed freeze.

I note the bare head on the turkey, and the wattle hanging down; it would seem the wattle would freeze. Is it insulated in some way? Is the entire head, which seems to be bare, also insulted? The ability of creatures to withstand extreme cold is always interesting.

At Home in the Woodlands

A red squirrel comes out and challenges a gray for a morsel of food. But although the red is normally a feisty rascal, the two seem content to bury the hatchet on this cold morning and eat, side by side.

Do I remember hearing something to that peaceful effect among humans in the far north? Did white explorers in the far north discover the Eskimo people (or Inuit, as they call themselves), to be a relatively peaceful people?

It is certainly true that you don't hear of Inuit tribes lining up and going into battle against each other as we temperate-zone folks do, leaving thousands of our kind dead on the fields of battle. Could this "icebox effect" be a possible avenue to world peace?

A jet-black crow now sails in and joins these two bushy-tailed rodents and invites them to share whatever road kill or something else they have discovered. These three make quite a picture.

Black crow and his brothers had just been complaining about a predator or something in the area. All we need now to complete this picture is to have a big buteo hawk swoop in and join the road kill feast. But perhaps even the icebox effect has its limits. You'd likely have to put crow and hawk into the deep freeze for a spell to get them to be peaceful.

The raucous bedlam of crows moves in the direction of the river. One of the area birders, Rich Roehrdanz, informed me that crows will often gather and harass predators, and the bedlam will often attract other crows, who join in the din. This commotion of many crows is usually a signal that that is what they are up to.

In the Yukon, we experienced ravens. I learned then that ravens and crows tend to be territorial and drive each other out of the area, so that you seldom see them both in the same area, which is helpful for identification.

One knows, of course, that the ravens are bigger, but such information is useless, because I can never get them to sit side by side for comparison. So the territory factor is more useful to me. The ravens were a source of constant amusement in that north country. They would sit atop the lamp posts in downtown Whitehorse and burble away at us below with their nonsense chatter.

If an open pickup parked below them, they would wait until the owner walked away, and then they would glide down and check out the truck box for possible food. If you put food out for your dog in a dog dish, they would come down in pairs. One would tease the dog away from the dish, while the other would steal its food. They didn't seem to mind people at all but just cocked their heads at you and eyed you as if tolerating your presence among them.

One day my old black Labrador retriever, Lady, lay down in the middle of the road in the snow in front of my place and took a snooze. Several ravens glided down and took a couple of pecks at her to check her out as possible carrion.

Lady was highly-incensed at being so mistakenly considered, but she was too old and too arthritic to do more than scoot them away a few feet with snaps and snarls. The ravens finally grew tired of the game and figured they'd have to wait awhile for her to become a suitable dinner and flew off. Their great black bodies lifted up off the ground, and they soared out of sight over the treetops.

However they had yet another gambit that was the cutest trick of them all. We had photoelectric cells on the tops of our street lamps that turned them on in the evening. Raven learned that if he sat on top of one of those cells, he would turn on the lamp and he could hunker down and warm his bottom very cozily in subzero weather.

Most of all I learned that if they came upon a fresh kill or a carcass in the forest, before taking a bite, they would call in their brothers to share in the feast, and they would help guard each other from predators as they ate. It reminded me of the similar cooperation I had seen in the crows down south in North Dakota and Minnesota.

Now suddenly I see a great horned owl sail across in front of me, along the length of the river ice; the white flash on its side and the square shape of its head identifying it. The crows are in hot pursuit. The willingness of crows and ravens to act corporately rather than as selfish individuals is quite remarkable. This reminds me so much of wolves in that way.

Speaking of our predator friends, the great horned owl has frequented the river bottoms this past week on these extremely cold nights. He has made himself evident with his five-note call.

He offers a rather haunting picture on such nights. With only a new moon to light the sky and trace the bare silhouettes of the great white oaks and green ash against that sky, and the night completely silent otherwise, the low hoot of that great owl sounds like an ominous warning to any small rodents that might be out and about to scurry for cover — for that owl-eyed phantom is on the prowl and will likely see you before you see him.

The owl has landed in a big tree across the river, trying to unruffle his dignity. The crows have left him in peace, seemingly satisfied with having driven him out of state.

****

Winter has deepened, and winter wind under a completely overcast sky, covered with high, forbidding altostratus clouds.

A few snowflakes appear, followed by a sudden snow squall. Now they have disappeared, and only the wind remains, tossing a few brown oak leaves around over the barely snow-covered ground.

Happily, the wind is a south wind, gradually raising the temperature from the subzero degrees it has reached over the past few days. It's amazing how the wind penetrates hood and mackinaw and gives the lie to warming temperatures.

I catch sight of a flock of several dozen turkeys to my left and behind me. They seem fairly undisturbed by humans. I become curious as to how near they will let me come to them, if I move slowly and gently in their direction. They don't seem flustered by my advances, but they drift slowly ahead of me, keeping 30 yards or so between us. Occasionally one will pause, stretch up his neck and eye me. Is he curious or does he feel responsible for the group?

This week my Audubon friends informed me that the feathery tufts I see on the chests of some turkeys is called a beard. That was disappointing; I thought it had a much more auspicious name than that. They also tell me that it indicates the bird is a tom. They have moved away behind me now, out of sight.

The North Dakota Department of Forestry has placed a sign near a large tree. It announces, "North Dakota's Largest Silver Maple Tree. Posted 1997."

This strikes me as interesting, because I was not so aware of the silver maple growing in this area.

The tree is not extremely impressive, having two trunks that rise from a single base. But on closer examination, I see the remains of a huge trunk that has broken off at the base.

It is not a very shapely, attractive tree, as one sees in illustrations of trees, which is a bit of a disappointment. We humans expect a "largest tree" to live up to some kind of museum standard.

Perhaps this maple's looks have been damaged by the deterioration of age (as aren't we all), with a little help from a couple of big windstorms. And it is in its non-plumage season of the year. But it does measure an impressive 24 feet around its base. So it obviously had been lordly in its day.

The rare experience is to be able to identify such a tree as a silver maple in the winter, when it has no foliage to assist in the identification. What can I learn from this experience to help me in future experiences like this? It has a flaked bark, compared to the ribbed bark of a big old cottonwood nearby (that measures 27 feet at the base) or the neatly-corduroyed bark of a white ash a little further on. I do find a few old dried-up leaves under each to help in identification.

Now my turkey friends have appeared again behind me, moving up alongside me, eight or 10 yards to my left. They are training me to remain still if I want to enjoy their closer company. Audubon writer Ryan Lynd tells us, "In order to see birds it is necessary to become part of the silence." Perhaps that will always be true. These great birds move almost silently among the trees, with only an occasional gobble to betray their presence.

The ash woods along the river were entirely still at first. Then suddenly they were alive — the whole of the upper terraces of the forest churned and whipped, as if a spirit moved among them. A biting cold east wind blows across the river. The temperature stands at several degrees below zero.

Now, as suddenly, the woods are still again, as if whatever spirit stirred them has passed on from here. The Greeks have a word for spirit that translates as "breath." And it is, perhaps, a good one, as if that breath breathes upon the land from time to time and transforms it in different ways. I might argue that it is always life-giving, in a way.

Day by day, the days grow longer during these months. Oh, I know it is only by small increments that it happens here in these temperate zones, but it is the feeling that comes from knowing that that stirs something inside of us. The breath-wind and the day lengthening are like something alive, even in the stillest cold of winter.

We lived for a time in the Yukon, and there I remember that after the winter solstice, the days went rushing on madly toward the summer solstice. Whereas here by the Red River, the days change at a minute or two at the most, there they race on at a wild 11 minute a day change. For, of course, they must rush on from the great darkness in December to a midnight sun in June.

Last week I wondered about the dark forms of two birds among the trees on the riverbank and supposed they might be either starlings or grackles. But I felt I must check the Christmas bird count for this area to see if those two are, indeed, here.

On inquiring, I discovered that the grackle was seen not at all. So he has definitely flown to warmer climes.

But the European starling presented himself over 10,000 times; 19 times on the Minnesota side of the river and the rest on the North Dakota side. So the starling was a good candidate for what I saw last week. But today, if he is holed up in the hollow of that tree down yonder, he is not favoring me with a look at all.

The Christmas bird count is too numerous to recount to you here, but is truly an amazing list totaling 59 species; more than the 54 that I estimated last week, and 11 more than the 48 we've seen the past few years. But to name a few, we saw three species of ducks (plus a goose), seven of hawks (plus a bald eagle), four of upland game birds, four of owls, 34 of insectivores (most of them our beloved song birds but not singing this time of year) and a number of others. One that did not show himself the day of the count but that several of us had seen on previous days is, amazingly, the bluebird.

The wind-breath has mostly settled down now. I remember that at Leech Lake we could often have a crashingly-windy day and the evening would often settle that wind down to a great quiet. So it does this evening and says, 'Good night."

****

A blizzard was forecast to blow in the Red River Valley from 6 a.m. to 6 p.m. today. Yet, at 6 a.m., everything looked bright and cheery and calm. At 9 a.m., the same. The weather is having trouble agreeing with the weatherman again. And all public events have been busy cancelling themselves for the occasion.

The snow lies deep upon the land. It is what you would call a quiet, beautiful winter day.

A white-breasted nuthatch disturbs the motionless quality of the woods by zipping across my line of vision and landing on a green ash tree. He inspects the bark, and then disappears into the woods.

And now, believe it or not, a winter robin flies in, hovers a bit and then lands in an ash tree not 12 feet in front of me. He looks as if he might roost there a bit, but then another robin joins him and they fly off together. Normally they seem to like berries. Are they finding berries or seeds of their choice in the woods?

I claimed the other day that I had seen the red-cockaded woodpecker. I took up the case with my Audubon friends, and they assured me that that Southern bird (Georgia and South Carolina), I would not be seeing up here. Several of them have seen that bird in field trips down in those states.

They did, however, take an interest in the distinctive s-r-e-e-p sound that I had been hearing and said they had heard the starling make a sound like that. And indeed, the bird authority Peterson indicates that the starling is capable of that sound. They tell me the starling is a great imitator and is known to ape a variety of sounds from other birds.

The day is strange. Earlier a suggestion of sunlight appeared in the east, and then disappeared. The sky became completely overcast and seemed to suggest an approaching storm.

Then blue sky appeared and the sun came out. Now a light dusting of snow is falling. A little wind is picking up. A predicted blizzard is four hours late, but it appears it could come. I think it is time for me to seek a warm fireside.

****

A light fluffy snow falls gently and all of the woodland creatures seem to be hunkered down except the squirrels, which seem to like the snow.

I've always been curious about squirrel tracks, which seem to suggest that squirrels run backwards, planting their hind feet ahead of their front feet, rather like a hunted creature trying to fool a tracker. Of course the idea of running backward is ridiculous unless you are a crab (and I've always wondered how a crab can see where he's going), Now I look for a chance to see a squirrel making his tracks to see why they appear so.

While the squirrel moves so swiftly your eyes cannot "stop-camera" his actions, his newly-made tracks tell the tale. He does indeed place forepaws on the ground, compact his body into a ball and swing hind legs ahead of his body and plant them onto the ground. Maybe, when I think about it, all four-legged animals do that when they are running and even we do that when we are playing leapfrog.

A difference, if we were to note any, is that the timid creatures, like squirrels and rabbits, are usually on the run, while the larger creatures don't need to. They have the leisure to walk along in a lordly fashion.

A beautiful pileated woodpecker flashes across my line of vision and lands high up in a green ash tree, 40 feet in front of me. He checks out the bark with a couple of whacks, then, to my delight, he flies over to a giant dead American elm tree and lands directly above me.

Then, if I hadn't watched him closely, I wouldn't have seen him disappear into a six-inch hole on the underside of the tree trunk and refuse to reappear to confirm my observation.

I say "underside" because the tree lists at a 60 degree angle, offering an ideal protected underside away from rain and wind and snow. He was snugly settled in for the night, if he planned to remain there.

I've often wondered, in observing nesting places inside of trees used by birds, how they escape being flooded by rain in a heavy downpour, and if they carve their homes upward, once they entered the trunk of the tree.

I've seen a rock dove or pigeon make a home in such an opening, year after year. He seemed to get along and helped raise his brood each year.

Of course another engineer would have had to construct the home, like a woodpecker or squirrel, as a dove is ill-equipped for such work. But the dove is brassy enough to move in on the home when it is empty and take it over. So it makes an ideal home for him.

At Home in the Woodlands

Now I observe that the pileated woodpecker constructs his home neatly on the underside of this giant elm. He could have built it on any side of the tree, and indeed he would have had gravity in his favor on any other side. Does he know by instinct that this side offers him ideal protection from the elements?

I suppose that Darwinists would tell us that birds don't calculate these things, but they know them somehow in their make-up. All birds without this "knowledge" in their make-up quickly got flooded out and went extinct. And all birds with this "knowledge" carved their homes out of the lee side of a tree, and they survived and thrived.

However, like the time traveler in H.G. Wells' "The Time Machine," perhaps I will draw this brilliant conclusion, only to discover later that I am completely wrong. (Sigh!) We human animals are limited to going from conclusion to conclusion and muddling along the best we can.

I hope the woodsman will spare this old elm tree until some storm finally takes it down. Who knows how many homes there may be in that wonderful big old denizen of the woods? I see another four-inch hole higher up on the same trunk, likely another home for some resident who doesn't mind a pileated for a neighbor. Well, at least for tonight, rest well, my woodpecker friend.

****

A friend remarked to me this week an experience that demonstrated the smartness of crows. A group of crows in captivity were tended by persons who wore a unique mask. Later, when the crows were released from captivity and someone else would wear that mask in a group of people, the crows would dive-bomb that person, recognizing the mask.

I'm not sure that incident represented or demonstrated a great deal of intelligence, but I have been impressed with the ability of their cousins, the ravens, to cooperate rather than compete with one another.

I recall one fellow who came upon a fresh deer kill, apparently left by wolves in the Yukon, when I lived there. The ravens, who usually arrive soon after a kill, had not yet arrived.

So seeing an opportunity to observe them, this man set up a quick blind and waited. Sure enough, soon a single raven arrived. One might have expected that raven to quickly dive in, gorge himself and depart. But no. He provided a lesson that humans could benefit from. After cocking his head and eyeing the kill and the surroundings sagely — including the blind, while the watcher held his breath — the raven began his raucous call. Soon other ravens answered him and before long, a flock of them gathered.

However even then he did not rush in for the first pickings at the carcass. Two or three others joined him on neighboring branches as watchers, presumably for other scavengers that might come and disturb them, while the others went in to eat. Soon relief watchers flew up to take over the guard duty while the first watchers flew in to join the feast.

Mealtime progressed in a fairly mannerly fashion; no bickering or scrapping over dainty morsels. It happened on this occasion that no other scavengers arrived to disturb them. After a time, as if on a prearranged signal, the ravens flew up and disappeared over the treetops. The watcher folded his blind and walked away to report his observations.

I am led to realize that I have a lot to learn about these corvids. On a quiet early summer when one decides to perch above my tent and bellow out his raucous cawing, I consider the world could well do without them. But perhaps in time I shall be indebted to them for what they can teach me.

****

Heavy snow showers and blustery winds greet me in the woods today. Crows seem to be the lone representative of wildlife braving a building winter snowstorm. Everything else seems to be hunkered down for the duration.

Suddenly 11 wild turkeys make a liar out of me. They scamper by, 80 yards away, stopping where they have scraped away the snow and seem to have found something edible. They seem undaunted by the weather conditions.

Actually we're experiencing only the vestiges of a storm. They've predicted a big storm, but the weather has a way of not cooperating with the weatherman in these parts. A little snow fell in the night, and light wind from the east has festooned the east side of all trees in the area. The woods are really quite lovely.

At first I thought from the lack of fresh tracks that there was nothing out and about this morning. I saw plenty of turkey tracks and some deer tracks, but a light snow falls continually, so I thought they might be from yesterday.

We humans were getting storm predictions; panic had set in and events closing: churches, Sunday schools, church dinners, concerts and the like. I thought of staying in myself but by morning, the temperature was 30 degrees, and it looked like just another winter day.

The mildness causes a wetness that is probably more hazardous for woodland creatures than the cold. I do not envy them getting soaked down and then trying to keep warm. Rabbits and squirrels seem smart enough to get into snug holes and burrows and stay put.

The heaviness of the wet snow seems to weigh down the spruce and bushes. A slight wind comes up, and they use the opportunity to try to shake free of their wet, heavy burden, but to no avail. The wind quickly dies down, and they peer out a bit dolefully from under their load at the white, wet world around them. They keep a dry spot of ground at their base that would shelter a passerby.

Even the turkeys have forsaken their grazing spot for the shelter of the woods now. To what place have they gone? Were I a bit more ambitious, I would trek over and see where they have bedded down. I shall use the excuse that I do not want to disturb them.

No, I do see two of them, huddled in the snow to my left. They fluff their feathers a bit once in a while and then tuck their heads in a little. They seem to have the ability to telescope in their necks and pull in their heads close to their bodies to wait out the bad weather. Their feathers shed water.

The snow falls steadily now. All creatures have settled in to wait it out. The turkeys have found the dry spot under the big spruce.

At Home in the Woodlands

****

What a treat to be enjoying a belted kingfisher winging its way across my line of vision, just eight yards in front of me. No, he hasn't lost his way and become trapped in the harsh winter of the white north. Instead, I'm taking a leave of the North's winter and am visiting the Los Angeles area.

How does one find woods in a large city? Surprisingly, humans — despite their development of mega-sized cities — seem to crave nature enough to retain patches of woods even in the midst of metropolitan areas.

New York's Central Park is a case in point, hosting a small forest in an area that is likely some of the most commercially-valuable real estate on the planet. Developers would love to get their hands on that land. Yet, somehow citizens have sustained the desire and political will to prevent that.

Los Angeles, it seems, is no different. Two short blocks from a busy commercial and residential area in Lake Balboa, a community that greater Los Angeles now encompasses, you will find an area of woods and waterways that give you a welcome relief from the busy urban activity surrounding it.

I settle in this area near a little waterway. The kingfisher skims above a tiny stream in a wooded piece of land and lights in a tall willow on the far bank.

I say "far," but it's a misnomer. The stream is no more than five yards wide, both banks covered in willows in their winter nonplumage.

That is not to say that L.A. is not green in winter. As I look about me in these woods, I see greenery everywhere on lower bushes. In residential areas, lawns are green, and we pick delicious oranges off trees in the yard. Even these willows sport fuzzy green blossoms.

Now the kingfisher sails by again, headed in the opposite direction. What is he hunting? Does his presence indicate the little stream supports some sort of water life that could make a kingfisher lunch, frogs or small fish?

The stream empties into Lake Balboa nearby, for which this community inside greater LA is named. All of these communities make up the San Fernando Valley and one of them is a name we all know: Hollywood.

My son, Rich, who lives a few blocks from here, informs me that in earlier years this area was not built up with houses because it was lower and would flood in winter. Now they have channeled the water off to the ocean.

As I approach, three ground squirrels scurry about in front of me and dive into holes, of which they have plenty. They seem to have been busy digging holes everywhere.

Rich tells me a large hawk has taken up residence here — it seems to be the red-tailed hawk — which has a regular daily source of ground squirrel lunches. Such a predator could account for the squirrel's numerous entrances to its home, as he has become a "frequent flyer" into the nearest hole when a hawk appears. I expect a few hapless ground squirrels had to become the sacrificial lambs when the hawk first appeared to teach the others caution.

At Home in the Woodlands

The ground squirrel has made me curious. Is this the Richardson ground squirrel that frequents the prairies of North Dakota? I would have to check on this.

Now suddenly things get lively here. A phoebe lands on a willow branch about a dozen feet to my left. It cocks its head a bit and then flies off. Immediately a snowy egret flies in with a frog or something in its beak. Nuts! If I had seen his approach and frozen, he would have landed on the bank a few yards in front of me and had his lunch. He started to land, but I moved a bit, and he saw me and departed.

Now there's a show! A small hawk, perhaps a Cooper's, chases a kingfisher not ten yards in front of me above the surface of the stream. The kingfisher announces their approach with some wild screaming, which alerts me, and I see the whole chase as it goes by. For some fortunate reason, the hawk gives up the chase and sails back in front of me above the willows on the other bank. Another kingfisher lives to tell his cousins what a scare he had today.

****

Groundhog Day finds me back in the great white north. I haven't seen the groundhog today, but it is a bright and sunny day, and if he came out he has certainly seen his shadow and gone back into his hole; and we are in for another six weeks of cold weather. We've had two months of it already, so six more weeks of this cold is not a happy prospect.

As I look about me, the scene is bright from the sun shining on a thick blanket of snow on the land. It is not an unpleasant sight, just cold. The cold nips at you around the edges of your parka as you step out into it.

A red squirrel greets me about 200 feet in front of me. He sits up on a stump and nibbles away at something he has discovered. Then he suddenly pops out of sight into some nearby bushes.

A turkey comes up from the river bottom to check out the terrain to see if he can discover something — something edible, I suppose. Is there anything else that is interesting to him, except that which is edible or is sex?

Sometimes I think there is a third interest. When it is a warm day and everything is freshly green, and a comforting sun shines down upon it all, I see them just hunker down in all of this freshness and warmth and soak it all in. A third interest they may have is that which is pleasant.

A single young whitetail deer comes up from the river bottom about 150 feet in front of me. He has not discovered me yet. Now a second and a third join him, and now an older one who is a bit of a bully. Now one has discovered me and stands looking straight forward at me.

It is a curious thing that a deer will stand looking straight forward at me, while a turkey and other creatures stand sideways to me and gaze at me with one eye. Why?

A recent TV nature program gave a study of the whitetail deer. It suggested the deer is almost blind by human standards but has a remarkable sense of hearing and smell. That suggests that the deer is focusing not his vision but his hearing and smell on me, tipping his ears forward as he gazes at me.

I am curious to know what the deer is experiencing. Is he perhaps detecting even the breaking of a twig or a shuffling in the snow on my part that I am not even aware of? And does he have the patience to stand and gaze for a long time in my direction, waiting to discover if he can hear another sound from the direction he first heard some noise? It seems one could live for a long, long time with these marvelous creatures and still discover there is more to know about them.

The sun has settled to a low slant in the sky and begins to cast long shadows. The cold has begun to seep in more and more around me as the day lengthens. It is time to go.

****

Later, I return in daylight to enjoy this winter scene. A white-tail doe to my right surprises me. I move a little, so she spots me before I see her. I have just a moment to spot her movement before she freezes among the winter stand of green ash trees.

She eyes me for a few minutes and when I seem to pose no threat, she moves ahead among the trees. I look away for a moment and when I look back, she has disappeared.

I look at the exact spot where she should be and wait for a slight movement to give her away. A flash of her white flag tail; a flick of her ears. It is maddening.

I train the glasses on her. No luck. She blends beautifully with the winter trees, and she knows it. And she knows enough to remain still.

Then a yearling comes toward her from the other direction and gives her away. They move off together away from me, out of sight.

Such silent creatures they are, moving like ghosts through the woods and blending so perfectly with their surroundings. They have certainly learned the art of disguise. A predator would need their scent to discover them at such times. And they say that the young fawn is without scent for its first month; a further disguise.

A downy woodpecker flits across my field of vision and lands in a tall tree. I expect he will begin whacking away at the tree trunk in his usual manner, but in a moment I discover that he must have disappeared into a trunk hole about 30 feet above the ground. The trunk of the tree forks just below that point, and this fork is entirely dead. I see another hole a foot above the first, and a third just below those two; and far above, yet another. Perhaps that section of tree would boast more homes if I took the time to search. What a bonanza.

The river ice is solid from the cold weather, even though it is open for a patch below the spillway. It will take a good spell of subzero weather to ice that over. For a century we had a spillway across the Red River near downtown Fargo-Moorhead. But the roiling water beneath the dam resulted in at least one death a year for a number of consecutive years. For safety's sake, some years ago the spillway was replaced with huge rocks, and is now a small rapids.

The thick ice has given me a chance to walk on water and check out the span of the river. I find it is 60 yards across to the Minnesota side and 55 yards a mile downstream where I sit in warmer weather.

At Home in the Woodlands

That span is not so great as rivers go, but it is enough to be the largest source of a potable water supply for a metropolitan area of over 200,000. Continued city growth will no doubt require an additional water supply from the west in the future, but for the present, this ancient remnant of old Lake Agassiz will suffice.

The Red River carries a great deal of silt from off the fields upstream, so it always puzzled me how they could pipe potable water from such a stream. It took a class in microbiology for me to learn this.

I audited such a class at NDSU years ago. Not being a scientist by nature, I thought the class would be a study of little animals (forgetting, of course, that microbes are little animals, too). At one point the prof took us on a field trip inside the city water plant, and I saw the incoming water from the river — awful, putrid-looking stuff, and the outgoing water for our city system — as pure and pristine-looking as you please, a miracle of modern technology.

Gray-blue wings sail into a cavity high up in the bole of a tall red maple nearby. It is the rock pigeon, so common in many areas it seems hardly worth mentioning, but unusual to see nesting high up in this tree in this wooded area.

Who will even bother to mention this bird, as if it were some domestic fowl gone feral? Perhaps that is what comes of being common.

I remember that, back in western Minnesota where I grew up, to us boys they were just plain old "pidgins," a common sight around any farmyard or town elevator. They were just around; not important. They lived so hand in glove with people that, now and again, one of the boys would keep some of them as pets.

Although we weren't farming people, we lived out on a farm near town for a time, surrounded by a farmyard, complete with barn. I recall one day when I was alone at the place, a young man knocked on the farmhouse door and asked if he could go up into the hayloft and get some of the squabs. Although at that time I didn't know much about birds, I did know the squabs were pigeon young, which suggests it must have been common knowledge around there. I said, sure, go ahead. And that also suggests the indifferent opinion we had of pigeons in that farming area. Perhaps one needs to raise them to have some kind of respect and fondness for them.

We moved out to central North Dakota in our early married life. We had lived there for several years before it struck me that, going about the countryside from farm to farm in my work, I had never seen a pigeon. Later I saw a few, but obviously they preferred the corn country.

Still later I took an interest in them and began to study writings about them, especially after seeing virtually thousands of them in the city squares of great cities like New York and London. I discovered they are descendants of an old bird species called the rock dove of the order Columbae, which species, as I understand it, still exists in some parts of the world.

Anyone would look at rock doves and say, "Aw, that's just a plain old farmer's pigeon." And he would be right.

I remember a few years ago, wondering about this ubiquitous bird and why it never made it into bird books. So

At Home in the Woodlands

I checked our most famous authority, Roger Tory Peterson, to see what he had to say about old Columba livia.

Under pigeon he says, "see dove, rock." And under rock dove, he has just three lines: "This bird has become feral and in some places, it is as firmly established as a wild species as the house sparrow or the starling. It needs no description."

Even today I see our common bird listed as rock pigeons in bird counts.

However he obviously has lost a lot of his old respect. My naturalist, Hornaday, writing in 1904 in his section on Columbae, doesn't even mention him, nor does Ashbrook's "Birds of America." I'll have to check my Roger Tory Peterson on birds, which is where I must have read about him.

Now I have observed the rock pigeon fly into this same maple tree bole in the spring and early summer during the nesting season and raise her brood and apparently successfully launch them into life. It seemed an unusual place for her to be doing this, but it must have been safe enough from predators for her to succeed. And now I discover she has made it her winter home as well, and I wish her equal success in this.

****

The sun slips over the tops of the maples to my right, ushering in the morning. I am sitting today in the old cemetery in Minnetonka, Minnesota, overlooking a willow-ringed frozen pond below.

The morning-glancing sun washes the new fallen snow among the graves between me and the maples with a brilliance that makes the snow almost impossible to look at without turning away to rest the eyes.

The maple and spruce woods around the area seem almost bereft of fauna. A lone chickadee fusses among the twigs in the big maple in front of me, and a single crow wings his way across the crest of the maples from east to west. Now they have both flown, and they leave me alone in the stillness.

I am left with the great trees, those quiet sentinels that faithfully guard us day and night, summer and winter, century upon century while humans, as Wilder puts it, "strain away' at this business of living. We strain away at the business of birthing and then burying our families in old cemeteries like this one. We work at buying and selling our homes, launching upon and then returning from our careers and finally, lying down to rest in quiet places like this, where these silent sentinels faithfully watch over us all that time and for all time to come.

When the winter woods grow silent, one is much more aware of these great trees that we take so much for granted in the summer, when birds and mammals entertain us. These are the months when their soughing whispers to us, "We are here. Stop to look at us for a moment. Lean against us, if you will. We are strong, and we will hold you up. And when at last they plant you in the ground like us, we will nestle you among our roots safely for years to come."

Two human passersby, the Haugos, have just stopped to chat. They inform me that in a month I would not be up to my eyeballs in water, it would be over my head. They've hiked this route weekly for 35 years.

The great ash, maple, elm, basswood and oak trees along this river stand as sentinels to the flood each year. The riverologists tell me that as long as the river rises and recedes before the sap rises in the trees, they are safe. But if it flooded in a later season, it would kill them. I'll need to look into that further, for surely there are floods in warmer climates that don't kill all the trees.

To my delight, a red-bellied woodpecker sailed in and began hammering on a white ash tree not 15 feet to my left. He's flown off now, but hopefully he'll come back.

Three sparrows flit among the upper branches of another ash tree. Is it possible the song sparrow is here this late? He has the familiar black spot on his breast.

And now two downies have flown in and are worrying bark on a young ash that arches in front of and above me. In fact they are so close that they are flicking pieces of bark down onto me.

Now it's more downies, nuthatches, chickadees, sparrows, you name it. And I hear the familiar kuk-kuk of the hairy woodpecker nearby, who can't seem to work without voicing himself a bit as he does so. As I sit still, the birds are flitting back and forth in front of me. I wonder what it must be like in the migration season when warblers are coming through. Then the thicket would be leafed out and I would be quite hidden.

Soon two slate-colored juncos appear in a nearby ash. One of them swoops down into the little bramble bush not 10 feet in front of me. He cocks his head and eyes me sagely, then flies off.

Before long, two of them are dashing back and forth through the dense woods in front of me, chasing each other. It boggles my mind how they can flit through the dense branches so swiftly and not bump into them.

And look at that! There are two cedar waxwings about at eye level, 25 feet off to my right! Beautiful! I see a lot of berries on the bushes for good feeding.

I become curious about the tree life in this thicket. I continue to remark on the white ash, but they are not necessarily dominant here. Although the trees are bare of foliage, there is no snow on the ground, and I have the observation advantage of a good bed of brown leaves under each tree.

Both the red and white oaks are well represented here; beautiful big, stately trees. I expected to see some maple, as I know they are plentiful in the Cities, but I don't see them in this copse of woods. It makes me wonder if trees are territorial — the oaks are saying, "This area belongs to us."

Well, I am grateful that they abide a mere mortal like me, sitting among them for these few hours.

****

A small hawk greets me as I come to my place in the forest on the Red River today. Unfortunately he is not alive. He lies, wings folded and lifeless, alongside my path.

He is in such perfect condition that he takes my breath away; he looks almost as if he could come to life. I pick him up gently and turn him over in my hand. This is, for certain, the closest look I have ever had at a merlin. The last time I had even seen one was 10 years ago, but I see that they have been reported in the Christmas bird counts in this area almost every year for the last century.

As I sit down in the woods I quite marvel at the experience of having him so close in front of me. It is a rare opportunity one has to view such a bird so closely. He is frozen, of course, and nearly perfectly preserved, allowing me to observe and record each characteristic on my basic 15-point checklist.

I see black and white bands across the underside of his long, beautiful tail, his lack of an eye line, and the whisper of a white tip at the end of his tail feathers.

He is 13.5 inches long, and I note that we have only four hawks here that small; and one of them, the kestrel or sparrow hawk, does not get large enough even to match that length. So I limit the choices to three: sharp-shinned hawk, Cooper's hawk or merlin (pigeon hawk). Correctly speaking, the kestrel and merlin are in the falcon family.

A few days later, when I take it to an Audubon meeting for a kind of show-and-tell before the experts, I learn it is the sharp-shinned hawk.

A simple discovery by the Red River has given me a wealth of experiences.

The sky offers only stratocumulus overcast: a gray day indeed. I am supposed to be sitting in the middle of a fairly violent snowstorm that was to begin at about 4 a.m. It is now five hours overdue and provides us with only a gray day and a tiny breeze that gently disturbs the tops of the still-winter ash trees.

You have, no doubt, heard of the weather man who left an area after many years because the weather did not agree with him. I came out this morning, thinking I would scuttle back into shelter from the storm. It just isn't so.

However the woods are amazingly shy of animals this morning, except for that sparrow hawk; no deer, no wild turkeys in the places where I usually find them. Do they sense an impending storm better than I do, and do they find shelter to avoid it? Perhaps they are my best weathermen. Only a gray squirrel hopped across my line of sight a short time ago, but even he has disappeared.

Perhaps humans who live closer to the elements, like in the far north, learn to read the weather better than we southerners. I remember when we lived outdoors at Templar Point on Leech Lake, my wife became very good at reading the western sky over Walker for approaching weather systems.

One of the Audubon folks, Marshall Johnson, has kindly provided me with the latest Winter Bird count listing. It is always interesting to see what unusual bird visitors remain in winter, especially since winter seems intent on stretching into July this year.

I see the sharp-shinned hawk, a single visitor, appeared for this year's count. That alerted me to the possibility that I was seeing that hawk this morning, as the sharp-shinned has dull orange on it as well. But the coloring is on its breast, not back, as I observed.

****

At Home in the Woodlands

Audubon's Christmas Bird Count is underway all across America, at least in every city and town where there is an Audubon chapter or some other birder group. I began the day enjoying a cup of coffee with some family members and watching the dawn come in through an east window that looks out on my birdfeeders. I was curious when the first birds would arrive.

A chickadee arrived at the thistle seed feeder 15 minutes before sunrise and began his breakfast. But a moment later, a downy bombed in on the same feeder, and they frightened each other away.

A short time later, a flock of birds — nuthatches, finches, chickadees and woodpeckers — flew in and feasted awhile. They dined for half an hour, all departed for an hour, and then drifted back in ones and twos.

At the moment, I am doing my counting from the luxury of my woolly lawn chair on another gorgeous warm day that feels like the middle of May. We'll see if I can count a few birds from my post here by the Red River.

Actually I should say that we did go out and hike about and did a serious bird search this morning for a couple of hours before church. In that area during that time, we scored three downy woodpeckers, six white-breasted nuthatches, three crows, seven chickadees and four rock doves

Two crows have flown leisurely overhead and disappeared, heading southwest. Suddenly a strange phenomenon appears on the river. I could have sworn that the water had receded and rows of weeds and grasses appeared in the middle of the stream. Occasionally it is only reason that can surmount the evidence of the senses.

What I am seeing is that a film of water has appeared on the surface of the frozen river, due to this warm weather. The grasses on the far shore are reflected completely realistically in that water. I have not taken leave of my senses.

This weather is unbelievable. I am sitting here very comfortably, writing with bare hands just three days before the winter solstice. I am looking at winter flora all about me with none of the other trappings of winter — for example, snow.

The way this bird count works is that any volunteer can be out counting birds as I am doing this particular day. In our case, the city is divided into areas for record purposes. I and several others are counting in Area Four. Then at sunset, we all gather at the Spurbeck home for a potluck supper and we turn in our figures to Keith Corliss, who is the tabulator. Keith turns in the figures to the national office, which can then plot changes in bird populations and seek to find what is causing those changes.

Sometimes changes for birds signal changes for humans. Remember the canary in the cage down the miner's shaft? The death of the canary warned the miners of the presence of noxious gases. Tracking changes in bird populations can lead to discoveries that can affect lives of humans.

Darkness settles in upon the land now. It has been a beautiful winter day, with just enough snow upon the land to make it seem like winter, but not enough to make it troublesome.

At Home in the Woodlands

The woods have taken on the cloak of their night quietness. Only a cottontail scoots across an opening to my left. Why did he hurry so? Did another creature frighten him?

Now I hear the kak-kak-kak-kak of the pileated woodpecker. For a short time I do not see him, but finally he flashes across my line of vision to my left and lands on the big old dead cottonwood with big holes in it that pileateds seem to love. I hope they never tear down that tree.

The woods are quiet now. They are dark, but the whiteness of the snow continues the sense that light is still all about. It is strange. We know that whiteness is no more than reflection, but can we ever imagine a totally dark night in snowy woods? I can recall totally black nights in summer in the woods, where I could not see one foot stepping in front of the other. But in winter?

With night falling about us, most creatures conserve their warmth by retiring in this coldest part of the day. The cottontail likes the night, perhaps because he feels safest from predators. The owl likes it too, because he likes to eat the cottontail. Ah, that chain of life!

*****

Most years we take a winter trip to Ham Lake. Why? Who knows? Perhaps it's because of an urge to see the familiar summer flora in its winter garb. Perhaps we feel the urge to get behind cozy cabin walls, with a toasty wood fire in the stove to warm us after we've made our cheeks rosy with skiing, snowshoeing, or chopping holes in the lake ice.

In earlier years when our legs were younger, we'd venture to the lake even during winters with high snowfall; we would drive our car as close as we could to the cabin, and then haul our gear in with a toboggan.

In recent years, we've been able to take advantage of lower snowfalls and drive the car all the way down to the cabin. I say "down" because the approach road through the Norway pines descends to the cabin and lake. That makes the effort to toboggan gear back up the hill in deep snow a significant challenge.

A single gray squirrel scampers across the snow-covered ground about 20 yards in front of me here at Ham Lake on this winter morning. He has a bit of a job navigating the soft snow, but he soon reaches his destination of a tall Norway pine and scampers up it, no doubt in search of a tasty pine cone.

Nuthatches and chickadees flit about among the pines, seeking breakfast. Winter never seems to daunt them.

I've beaten the old sun at his rising this morning, but of course that is partly because we humans engage in the subterfuge of daylight saving time, or he would already be up. I see him lighting the far shore of Ham Lake already. I detect him now, just appearing through the pines behind me.

The snow lies in soft billows knee-deep across the entire forest and out over the lake. It falls in small amounts every day, and the accumulation is daunting for any foot-travelers through these forests. You sink nearly up to your knees on each step and have to stop every so often to rest, especially pulling a tub sled with gear on it, as I did coming in. Fortunately I had only a quarter of a mile to walk to the cabin. Extensive travel by foot in this snow would be exhausting.

Ah, there is old sun up in full bore now, warming the back of my neck. It is amazing how he creates a sense of warmth, even in this winter cold.

At first that sun made only a yellow glowing line on the far shore of the lake. Gradually that line advanced toward me across the lake until now it is only perhaps 300 yards out from where I am.

This bank remains still shrouded in the last vestiges of night, although some sunlight is breaking through the pines behind me, dappling the snow with its yellow glow. The west side of the reddish bark of the Norway pines in front of me has taken on the red-gold hue of the sun now as well.

Oh, look at this! A young whitetail deer has appeared on my left and is passing 15 yards in front of me. What a sight! He appears to be a yearling, which may account for why he is not cautious about detecting me. He passes a little to my right and then heads out to the lakeshore to check things out there.

Not much browse here, although there is some food in the low bushes to my left from where he came. At this age, however, is he out for breakfast, or is he just out for a frolic in the morning sun, like any youngster might do before beginning the serious business of the day and hooking up with mom again, wherever she is? Now he walks to the left and disappears again into the woods.

The morning quiet settles upon the land. The sun-shadow on the lake has crept almost up to my shore.

While skiing across Ham Lake the day before yesterday, JoAnn and I commented on why we were seeing so many deer tracks on the middle of the lake. Suddenly JoAnn stopped on the trail ahead of me and remarked, "There's the reason up ahead."

In the gathering dusk, my not-so-perfect eyes would have been hard put to identify what to me looked like some large object left out on the lake. But with a little study, I too could make out what looked like three deer standing very still at some distance from where we stopped and staring intently at us, having spotted us before we saw them. When we seemed to be unthreatening, they slowly began to amble obliquely away from us, stretching out into a group of six.

We continued our ski and a few minutes later, upon looking up, discovered they'd disappeared, evidently into the woods. Apparently they'd had enough of us.

What we pondered was what brought them so frequently (which was apparent from their many tracks) down on to the frozen lake. No food out there. No pools of surface water had yet begun to appear to offer a drink. Safety — a clear view of predators from a safe distance? That could only be wolves, it would seem, which were around too infrequently to even be a bother. The two-legged, gun-toting predators had long ago retired from the season. Perhaps it was just easy strolling, compared to the deep snow of the woods.

Back in the cabin later, before we had lit any kerosene lamps to betray our presence, JoAnn suddenly called to me, "Jim, come here quick — and quietly!" There, back of the cabin, not 15 yards away from our window, we saw a doe and a yearling standing still, with heads raised, staring intently at us through the windows. Through the darkened window, we were probably not even visible. Why are they always able to detect our presence more quickly than we see them? And why are humans not more frightening than we are? Perhaps we overestimate the awesomeness of our presence.

After a few minutes they lowered their heads and ambled away in a leisurely fashion, nibbling browse as they went. They were so casual. Of course permanent residents in these parts see deer so frequently in their yards that this is a ho-hum experience for them. But this was our first experience of having them right outside our windows. I'm sure that even old-timers will tell you that their first such experience was a thrill to them as well.

The two deer moved laterally around the house, browsing as they went, giving us this viewing feast for nearly half an hour before they wandered out of sight. The youngster acted quite independently, but we did notice that he was careful not to let too much distance come between him and mom. Typical teenager. Soon she'll have another, and she'll shoosh him away on his own. What a treat to see them.

****

When near home, my habit is to do my "over the dike" writing near the Red River on Sundays. Under the belief that one can find woods anywhere on the planet, wherever I may be, I find a place to settle on Sundays and write. Today, that "anywhere" is in Germany.

A dear friend from southern Germany, Martin Hoeschele, invited us over to his home to give us a view of Germany and a chance to have a good visit. This evening finds me in the famous Black Forest in southern Germany near Bad Liebenzell, which is near the city better known to Americans as Stuttgart. A distant church bell is chiming 7 p.m., and this February night in this forest is as dark as can be.

No, I am not finding my page from memory; I am aided by an artificial light. But the remarkable thing is that on this February night, I am able to sit outside and write with bare hands. I have to rub my hands together occasionally to warm them up, but it's tolerable. I can see my breath, but only slightly. The air is perfectly still, so no wind adds to the chill of the night.

The mountains rise around me on all sides, which perhaps protects me from any wind. The moon has not risen yet, and I recall it will be a full moon, so that has made the night very dark. I see the planet Venus above me amidst a field of stars. The heavens remain a constant the world over, at least on the same side of the equator.

But it does set me to pondering, if I had looked at that exact spot with concentration, would there are have been two precise moments, one in which Venus was not visible and the next in which she was? Perhaps Venus could appear in such a way.

There is a kind of magic in nature, isn't there? An owl greets me to start my evening, calling from up the mountainside behind me. He serenades me with an o-o-o-ooo, a call not quite familiar to me from North America. I was aware that I could expect owls here, but I suppose they would be a species new to me; so it seems I will need to study about them before I could identify them specifically.

My friend, Martin, remarked upon a giant owl he has witnessed in this area. He demonstrated its wing span by spreading his arms, suggesting a wing span nearly six feet.

At Home in the Woodlands

When I first thought about being "at home in the woodlands" for a few hours over on this side of the world, I wondered, "What shall I do to get any sense of what I might expect to see in the woods here, and how shall I identify them?" I decided to tackle just birds and trees alone and that would be enough to bite off for this venture in southern Germany. The heavens, thankfully, would be familiar territory, even over here. So I asked Martin if he would name for me a half dozen or so birds that the average person on the street might expect to see in Geislingen. I'd ask someone else about the trees.

Martin proved more than equal to the task. He came up with hawk, pigeon, sparrow, blackbird, chickadee, European robin, owl and sandpiper. And I would add crow to his list, as I see them all over.

For trees, I went to the tourist information center for help. The kind young lady at the desk and her colleague came up with Tanne, Buche, Eiche, Birke and Weide. When I looked dismayed, they also translated them into fir, beech, oak, birch and willow.

Something has flown overhead twice in the dark. The first time it had a sharp sound and the second time, a softer sound. What else could be flying out in the dark? Could it be they have the nighthawk here?

Whatever faint light from the fading day remained over the rim of the mountains has now faded away. The black of the night settles completely upon the Black Forest.

****

The trip to Germany now a fond memory, I find myself back home in the Red River Valley. As I mount the crest of a small ridge by the river, I suddenly become aware of a doe standing about 80 yards ahead and slightly to my right. She is standing broadside to me, with her head turned directly toward me, the two of us gazing steadily at each other as if to say — what? What do two creatures who do not speak each other's language communicate to each other?

I expect whatever it is we communicate is by body language alone. I heard her "saying" to me, "Are you a danger to me? Will you be advancing on me and pressing me to move away from this spot?" I stood for a long time in the new, deep, soft snow, making small movements but not moving from the spot. Perhaps she heard me "saying" to her, "I won't disturb you."

For a moment I am distracted by the pileated woodpecker flying into a nearby green ash tree and fussing about on one of the limbs, invading the silence with his kak-kak-kak-kak. He, no doubt, is headed for his tree home in the old dead elm nearby.

In that moment the doe has turned away a few steps, as if no longer disturbed by me. Then, to my surprise, four other deer rise up from the ground around her, which had been out of my line of vision in the brush. It is a bedding spot for them. The snow is starting to come down again in a light snowfall, and I am strongly tempted to go down and examine the spot before the snow covers it. But I desire not to disturb them. Perhaps I can see it another day.

Out of the corner of my eye, I spot the turkeys again, almost behind me, 22 of them. The light snowfall continues. I had wondered where and if they secreted themselves during a snowfall. That mystery will have to remain with them, for they are out foraging as if it were just another day. They are scratching the snow away in the search for food, snow that has accumulated to several inches now. They come surprisingly close to me if I do not move. If I make small movements they ease away from me a bit, but not with alarm.

I continue to be impressed with how these wild creatures adjust to living near us human creatures, who really are predators as much as any creatures are. We would like to believe they trust us, but I am wondering if they only feel some strength in numbers.

I was talking with an Audubon friend this morning and the subject of the saw-whet owl came up, which one bird guide described as absurdly tame toward humans. This friend said the same thing. You could almost go up to a saw-whet owl and pick it up. However, considering that owl's terrible talons, he would not advise it.

Darkness starts to settle in as the snowfall continues. Time for all creatures to go to roost.

****

The other day I went to the top of the dike by the Red River and took a longing look at the spot under the big elm among the tobacco weed where I sat in my comfortable lawn chair and watched monarch butterflies in the autumn before they went south. I realized in another month or so, if I sat there, I would have four or five feet of water over my head from the spring floods they promise us.

This quiet winter river with its small tracks will rise to become such a tide in so short a time. It is awesome to consider.

House finches, with their red and brown markings, have graced our safflower feeders again in the last few days after a long winter absence. It is good to see them again. Of course, the house finch is listed in the Christmas bird count, so those that I saw may be among those that remained for the winter. But I long to see the return of the migratory birds again. Those who prepare bird calendars record first arrivals in the first 10 days of March which, at this writing, is only two days away. Oh, happy day! The sun has begun to burn through already to touch dark spots on the forest floor.

Such migratory calendars, admittedly made for states further east of here, record already the arrival of robins, bluebirds and song sparrows in those first 10 days of March. One such calendar maker is John B. Grant, author of "Our Common Birds," an excellent little volume but old and likely out of print now.

A curious fact, however, is that birds were migrating in 1900, when Grant wrote, very much the same as they are in 2011. And they were robins, bluebirds and song sparrows (three that we haven't yet driven extinct) in 1900, the same as they are in 2011 and have been since the end of the Ice Age.

People and trees come and go, but the migrations continue like an old clock.

Red squirrel has secreted himself in his tree home now for the day. He has found a tree with several large broken-off branches and plenty of hollow spaces for nests. So he has nestled in his warm tree home to ward off the cold that will descend upon the forest again tonight, down to below zero.

Sleep well, red squirrel. The weather man promises that spring will eventually come.

****

Some moisture collected on all the winter branches last evening and in the night, the cold has garlanded them all in white with frost. You'll all recall we used to call that the work of Jack Frost with his winter paint brush. He'd have had a mite of decorating on all of those trees last night.

Now what strikes me is the lack of permanence in the woods — and in all the world, for that matter, I suppose. That big wild turkey sitting up in that maple tree is very important, as is the maple. And I, sitting down here looking at them, am very important, too.

Fifty years from now a whole other turkey will be sitting up there in a whole other maple tree, and they will both be very important. And a whole other person will be sitting down here looking at them through some radically-renovated binoculars and he will be very important, too. And a whole other downy woodpecker will be hammering away at a whole other ash tree nearby. And everything will be different. And everything will be the same.

I remember in the years on Templar Point on Leech Lake how I would come back, year after year, for nearly half a century to that small spot on the big lake. And every year, that spot would greet me with something different.

One year, the American redstarts were prominent on the Point. A few years later, they were gone, and they never came back.

One year a small floating island sailed down from the north end of Walker Bay and established itself on the beach near the high banks. It was impossible to budge by hand, and it looked as if it were there to stay. The next year, it was gone.

At one time there was little evidence of humans along the Point. Now they are evident all over the place. It makes me sigh a bit, but I realize I am being selfish. Things must be impermanent with humans, too, and what I was privileged to enjoy alone at one time, others must be privileged to enjoy as well in a changing world. And one day, I am gone like the redstart and someone else sits on the beach and watches the beautiful sunset in the west over the Bay.

And all things are different. And all things are the same.

****

Windless snow settles down upon the land around me. I say "settles,' because it doesn't seem to fall, only settle, growing deeper and deeper on the forest floor. I can tell the difference in depth even from last week as I wade about in the snow in my boots. Snowfall has, in a deceiving way, a kind of inexorable character; as if you stood out in it long enough, it would fill up the space around you and cover you.

The snowfall is sufficient now so that distant trees have become blurred into a white screen. I expect that if you were to watch that snowfall increase, that white screen would advance toward you until you were enveloped in white with zero visibility.

At Home in the Woodlands

The deer suddenly lope across my line of sight, 10 of them by now, having come up from the river. They circle around me and disappear off to my left. Hmmm. What was that all about? To say the least, they gave me the gift of quite a visual treat.

The snowfall continues. If it turned into a snowstorm, is one still at home in the woodlands? Is "at home in the woodlands in a snowstorm" an oxymoron?

If it became such a storm with snowbanks developing, and I could not see to move, it seems to me I would dig into the lee side of a snowbank and carve out a cavity large enough to sit in and wait out the storm. I am told one's body heat would keep the cavity from getting much below 32 degrees.

However, having opted for the lee side of the snowbank in my imagination, I am thinking there might be something to be said for the windward side. Would that not be better?

I recall coming down to our place on Leech Lake's Templar Point in midwinter in deep snow. I remember a little 4-by-4 foot storage building we had there, with its door facing the lake.

I wondered as I came nearer that day how I would ever get the door open in this deep snow. Upon arrival I discovered, to my delight, that the north wind off the lake had neatly split in front of the little building, lifting the deep snow onto either side and leaving the ground in front of the door as dry as a bone.

There is something to be said for the windward side of things in life. One can still be at home in the woodlands in a snowstorm.

James Alger

****

The experts tell us the shrikes, snowbirds and snowy owls begin to leave us to return north at this time. I have not seen the snowy owl here this season, but numbers of Audubon members have been seeing more than usual here this winter, which has been a delightful surprise.

The snowy owl has been a phenomenon this year in North America. For some reason, the lemming population has burgeoned; the lemming being a major prey upon which the snowy owl thrives.

So one thing leads to another, the snowy owl population has fattened up and multiplied. As I understand it, needing more territory, they have begun to move south out of the Arctic tundra. And "south" includes North Dakota and northern Minnesota. I hear that some of them have even been found down in Chicago.

A comic element in the advent of the snowy owl here is that everything here is new and they haven't been conditioned to fear anything yet. The human — what is that? So often they just perch and watch you walk by.

Where they come from, a tree is the black spruce, usually about 6-8 feet tall; the last tree at the northern edge of the tree line. The owl often lives beyond the tree line. Wide open spaces like O'Hare Airport in Chicago look like just the place for the snowy owl to set up camp; very like the open tundra. So they sit on open spaces and watch these big things called "airplanes" go racing by. Airport authorities have had to live trap them and transport them to other places so they don't get sucked into the turbines, a danger to both owls and planes.

So the beat goes on, of humans and other creatures learning to live next to one another. Seven young deer come up from the river bottom and stand staring at me, 100 yards to my left. Then 43 turkeys come up and join them. They've decided living with humans is not so bad, if humans behave themselves.

****

Today finds me above the banks of the Mississippi. A sharp-shinned hawk sails through the maple-basswood forest 100 yards ahead of me. He circles around through the trees to my left and finally dips below the high banks out of sight. I suspect he is searching for some winter critter that is abroad on this sunny March day that will make him a tasty lunch.

Far to my left the beautiful Shadow Falls drops perhaps 80 feet from the top of the high banks down into the Mississippi River. They might be called ice falls at this time of year, for although there is still a murmur of sound from the falls, they leave great stalagmites of ice on the bushes and trees on their descent in this winter weather.

The St. Paul Park System has kindly put up a written description of what I am seeing in the rocks along the falls for those of us who are geologically challenged. If one knew the rock timetable, one could count back through the millennia from the top of the falls down to the bed of the river today.

At the very top, of course, is the glacial drift, the stuff we putter around in, plant our gardens, mow our lawns and plant our cornfields. There we find some pieces of rock that we throw aside to make our soil more tillable.

Below that we see a very hard shelf of shale, now called Decorah Shale, that has survived the water-wear many, many thousands of years. The falls have only gradually worn it back.

The number of years represented in all this really boggles the mind. I need to represent them in the millions rather than the thousands, which is rather humbling as I stand and gaze at that shelf of Decorah Shale.

That shelf was laid down more than 400 million years ago, long before the glaciers that left the glacial drift. If I were able to take it apart, I would discover fossils of ocean creatures that inhabited those ancient seas, perhaps long before the first winged reptile ancestors of the sharp-shinned hawk sailed over these lands in search of the creatures of their age upon which they could prey.

Below the Decorah Shale, I can see the subsequent layers, the Plattville limestone, the Glenwood Shale, the sandstone with its caves and sharp cut-ins, and at the bottom the Shakopee rock layer, which takes one down to the Mississippi River bed. All of these water-worn cuts in the layers represent the recent history of this river channel, dating back a mere 10,000 years, after King David had already been laid to rest with his ancestors.

The limestone layers, hard and thick as it was, collapsed from erosion, leaving the shelf of shale overhanging above it to enable the waters of Shadow Falls to spill over it. Thankfully we have preserved the woods around the falls.

At Home in the Woodlands

The Mississippi River lies frozen from bank to bank. The Red River on the western border of Minnesota imitates it in this frozen aspect, both awaiting the end of a very cold winter. Thus the two rivers encompass the state of Minnesota in a ring of ice, not freezing it into immobility, but bidding it rest in this phase in the cycle of seasons in the North.

****

Fifteen white-breasted nuthatches greet me this morning, chasing each other among the branches of a white ash tree nearby and then capering off to a neighboring white spruce. And all things are the same as we start another day back at the Red River.

Yet they are different. Although a generous blanket of snow covers the earth here and the temperature is just below freezing, one can sense the land stirring. It is, after all, almost the middle of March, and the sun is longer in the sky each day.

The birder John Grant tells us that these early weeks of March are when we can expect robins, bluebirds and song sparrows to appear in small numbers. I usually look for a robin the first of April, but that isn't far away.

These are the days when places in the far north, like the Yukon, pass us up for length of days. Until now, their days have been shorter than ours, but each day they lengthen more quickly than our days and now they must rush on to offer a midnight sun by mid-June.

I am hardly moving in the woods, pausing to scan the woods along the river bottom with my binoculars, when I spot seven white-tail deer standing among the winter-bare poplar trees, gazing at me as if I couldn't see them. Something spooks them, and they bound away to my left for a short distance, but then they pause as if they were unruffled. Were they only led off on a gambol by one of their party who sparked them into frisking about a bit?

I notice that a tom turkey is ambling closer to me from behind. I turn very carefully and gaze at him. He stops his advance, cocks his head and eyes me, while I stand very still. He is very bold.

It occurs to me that my facing him poses a kind of threat. Very carefully, I turn completely around, still eyeing him from under the corner of my hood. Sure enough, he takes a few more steps toward me and then stops to scratch about in a shallow spot in the snow. It is as if I have become invisible by turning away. Perhaps I could learn the same lesson regarding the deer.

I remember the Scots telling me that we Americans are inclined to crowd the comfort zone of fellow humans and other creatures. Whereas the Scot is inclined to look politely down and away when passing you, the American is inclined to gaze boldly into your eyes. There is a kind of tender distance decorum that humans often don't have that is found among the woodland creatures.

****

I hear the unperturbed call of a crow in the distance, but otherwise the riverfront is cloaked in winter silence. Even the breeze has settled down and only slightly stirs the brown stalks of the white aster in front of me.

At Home in the Woodlands

Usually a bird has a reason for calling, but sometimes I suspect they just sound off for the heck of it. There is an old Chinese proverb that agrees with me: "A bird does not sing because it has an answer. It sings because it has a song." That will humble me a bit, when I call a bird and think I get an answer. He's likely just doing his thing. But it is great fun to think that I am having such a profound effect on the woods around me.

A small gaggle of nine Canada geese are just flying overhead. They are traveling fairly low, as if looking for open water. They honk a bit, just casually announcing their presence. They are a few among our thousands of geese that have wintered here this year; a product of our very mild winter.

Speaking of mild, I took the notion to come down to the riverfront with my chair and writing board for the first time in months. The big issue is whether the bare fingers can handle it, and they are doing quite well, thank you. I feel very like Dr. Zhivago. Do you remember the scene where he is writing poetry with fingerless gloves on, with the winter snows all about him?

One strange phenomenon this winter has been how few birds have appeared at our five birdfeeders all winter. Other Audubon friends report the same thing, and they surmise it is because there is so little snow cover on the ground; the birds are finding plenty of food without our feeders.

Curious about that food supply, I pluck a few stalks of bent-over wheatgrass near my chair. Indeed, one stalk still has 10 seeds on it this late into the winter. And the riverfront boasts thousands of these stalks. A goodly food supply. A downy flashes across the winter into the bug elm beside me. Has he a home here, and is he coming in for the evening?

****

A nuthatch chits away in the green ash trees across the river, but he refuses to be seen. Perhaps he will fly across in the time I am here and present himself.

Again it is one of those winter days that are so warm that I can sit outside with bare hands and write. February has been the only month this winter that I have been unable to do this. A phenomenal winter.

A black horsefly lands on my page, hops onto my index finger and up my hand, checking me out. She hops across to my other hand, and then away. A strange sight with snow all about me on the ground. From where has she come? From some warm house, where she's been holing up?

I obviously have a lot to learn about entomology. Is she getting broody, and preparing to hatch out her first brood of the season, with all this warm weather arriving?

I say snow all around, which is true. We have far more snow than Minneapolis, from which I've come today. But we also have great patches of bare ground.

Although ice still covers the river, with a covering of snow on top of it, the river has begun to flow a little above the ice near the river banks. It is pushing and nudging the land into springtime, as is the warm breeze and the bright sunshine. But the light snow cover enables the land to keep a last grip on winter, before winter is ushered out.

At Home in the Woodlands

Two crows fly overhead about 30 feet above me. They wing their way south, and then circle back north, remaining within my view above distant trees, flying together until they finally pass out of sight.

A moment later two Canada geese announce their presence, and fly over my head going southeast in a leisurely fashion until they finally disappear from my view. Does all of this pairing up mean what I think it means? All of nature seems to be urging the approach of spring.

Now two red squirrels are chasing along the riverbank about 20 yards in front of me. They head south, then after scrambling about a bit, they head back north past me again; the two of them very much an item, it would seem.

And now a special treat; a woodchuck is ambling along the bank on the far side of the river. I was able to spot him easily as his dark brown body passed across a patch of white snow.

I picked him up in the glasses and traced his journey for some time. If the river ice were sturdier I would love to go over and study his tracks.

What is he doing? He ambles up to the base of a half-rotted tree trunk, and I think perhaps he will go into it. But, after sniffing about it a bit, he passes on. He seems to be in no hurry and seems rather aimless in his wanderings, as if he has all the time in the world to check out the woods. Would that I could be so relaxed in studying the woods around me.

The woods and the river appear to be softening with the coming of spring. Water is gently flowing from under the snowbanks toward the river.

We are thankful that the weather remains cool and that the thaw slows as we anxiously anticipate the river floods again in the next few weeks. So far the river remains iced over, but it looks soft, with surface water by the south bank reflecting silhouettes of the riverbank trees.

The frequency of river floods has become a joke. Ten or 15 years ago, like during the big flood of 1997, the riverologists talked about hundred year floods. I don't hear that term anymore, as we're getting 100 year floods every year now.

We've filled more than three million necessary sandbags now, so we are ready and waiting to face the flood of 2011. The water will come up and cover the place where I am sitting and probably would be about up to my eyeballs, so I will have to retreat to higher ground.

For all our highly-skilled ability to control our own destiny, there is really nothing we can do about the river except abide it, since we have chosen to build our city right in the bottom of its natural flood plain. It will go on doing its age-old thing, perhaps long after we are gone from the earth. I wonder if the old river will remember with a smile the "age of humans," when we built our dams and dikes and diversions.

One of the factors in this flood control that we could not afford to be without is the willing volunteer student help from three colleges and the high schools in these cities. Student population changes every four years, and in the years when we used to spread out our floods and put a little distance between them, we'd be asking for one-time help from each set of students. Now the same students are coming out each year through their high school [and college] careers, which is even more admirable.

With an obvious sense of relaxation, we ease out of the winter. The furnace turns on less frequently. Woolen sweaters and trousers we clean and pack away.

Eventually we remove storm windows and gradually let that delicious outdoor air seep into our indoor lives. Before long we will fling wide open those windows, letting outdoors and indoors become one once again. We begin to feel a boundless sense of anticipation and release.

I happen to be a "cactophile," and I now ready my big planter boxes of cacti which have waited patiently indoors through the long winter until the wonderful day of transplanting into my rock garden, where they will soak up sunshine and occasional rain from May until October.

You must forgive us plant lovers — we are a bit of an odd lot who do strange things like talk to our plants. But I am convinced that just as much as my cacti love the spring rains after their winter "drought" inside, just as much they smile at breathing in the huge dosages of good clear, fresh air after months of stale indoor living.

These indoor plants that have huddled beside my radiators for half a year (cacti that I call my "Texas wimps") now go outside to join the four species of my tough North Dakota cacti that have weathered the winter cold buried under the snow in the rock garden.

Although we humans have become rather "wimps" ourselves since our hunter-gatherer days, most of us who live in the North stay to enjoy the winters for the brisk freshness of the wonderful season. Yet, we look forward to spring.

I want to say a parting word for the groundhog before we close him out for the season. I am told that he doesn't really hibernate, being one of the rodents in the squirrel family. Instead he fattens himself up good and settles into his den in October, comes out again on Feb. 2 and then, to complete the folk legend, if he sees his shadow, retires again for another six weeks of winter.

Apparently the little fellow saw his shadow last week. He was exactly on his six-week schedule for coming out. He had to cross a big snow patch last week, but he was the herald of spring as far as this week looks. Enjoy the warm spring days, old friend.

Chapter 4: The River Breaks Loose

Spring is upon us, like a new bride just entering the sanctuary that will introduce us to the wedding, which is summer. Spring commits us to a way of seeding and nesting and flowering and new seed-making and young growth that will realize full growth in the maturing of summer.

Sometimes we wish that the freshness of spring could stay with us forever. But that cannot be, any more than I as a human being can remain in the human population forever, or any more than I can remain young forever. And who would even want that — the acne, the voice changes, the angst of the search for belonging. Another young, strong generation can take my place in that struggle.

Perhaps it is a blessing that life is cyclical and not linear. The produce of mistakes tends to die off. And the produce of successes tends to reproduce.

I recall in grade school, we were asked to write an essay on our favorite season. I wrote about spring. There was something in spring that suggested the shedding of an old life and the donning of a new life. One day my pal, Bob Moffatt, came romping out of doors in summer shorts, while I was still clad in winter trousers. I had to rush home to correct my attire. There is a certain urgency about spring.

The first inklings of midday life in the woods are starting to happen, as the woodland softens with spring. The woods are coming alive. I'm hearing the first morning soundings from spring birds but not so many sightings yet. That will come in time.

Across the river I hear the hammering of a woodpecker — likely the downy or hairy, but it could be the red-bellied. We had a good viewing of the latter yesterday, with his bright red head at the top of a pole.

Above me in the ash tree, I hear the gentle murmur of a thrush. I whistle back, but he refuses to let me see him. There are no thrushes in the Winter Bird Count, except the robin, so it may well be a winter robin impatient for spring. Winter still holds its grip upon the land and the river here.

After a few days, this human has returned to the riverfront for the first time, after a very cold winter that stretched back to the first of December. It's good to be able to sit out with bare hands again among the still leafless willow stands, which are very red, and the tall remains of last year's brome grass, which offer a bright tan coloring to the woods floor along the riverfront.

A single crow calls out from across the Red River on the Minnesota side. He appears and sails up to the topmost branches of a tall ash tree and perches there majestically.

Soon an answering call comes from a crow over here on the North Dakota side. Of course they are no respecter of these human political boundaries and fly cavalierly across, wherever they wish.

The gray squirrels are out all over the place now, hunting for food on this almost-snowless ground. Of course they love these oak forests here and the abundance of acorns. Last year they produced such a bounty that we raked the acorns in bucketsful just to get them off the lawns.

Years ago here, I had set out on a vendetta to live-trap the squirrels in our yard and transport them many miles away. That was an adventure.

I was extremely successful in live-trapping them, usually baiting the trap with peanut butter. Almost every day I was putting a squirrel or two into the car and hauling it away.

When I reported this, folks would ask, "How do you know the same squirrels are not returning to your back yard?" Well, you have to respond to doubters in these parts, so I said, "I either captured 108 squirrels in my back yard, or I captured one squirrel who was a very slow learner."

The project did not diminish the amount of squirrels in the back yard. No, there are not 108 squirrels running around in the back yard at one time. There are only two or three of them on any given day, and they keep the rest away. However the project did give me and my grandsons a good eyeball-to-eyeball look at squirrels, including a few color aberrations and such.

The latest squirrel event is even more remarkable; I have to say, I've never seen the likes of it.

Occasionally a squirrel gets into our garage if I leave the door open for a few hours. Usually it's a small matter to chase them out.

This time it was a red squirrel, and he seemed unable to get away. I went up close to take a look and discovered he'd hooked his teeth into an old scatter rug and couldn't get himself loose. We pulled the rug out onto the floor, took a hedge clipper and cut him loose.

So if you see a cranky red squirrel come your way with a strand of rug cord hanging from his mouth, he hasn't been to the dentist like he should.

However, the sun cuts through brightly this morning and will continue to wear away the edges of winter today, as it has for several days. The river still lies frozen within its banks, but it looks ready to break through its coat of ice and swell. We are grateful for every day that the thaw comes slowly rather than in a mad rush.

Leafless trees, like silent sentinels, wait and watch with me. How patient nature seems at the moment. But I am sure Japan felt the impatience of nature when it saw the tsunami rushing in. Here, however, nature only stands quietly and waits for spring changes to come.

Each year I follow the annual contest put on by the Pilot Independent weekly newspaper of Walker, MN, to predict the day the ice comes out of Leech Lake in the spring.

It occurs to me that the ice-out on the Red River must happen at a moment. Having lived in several locations near the Red River for over three-quarters of a century — from its source at Lake Traverse to its mouth at Lake Winnipeg — I have never seen that moment. It seems like one day, we wake up and realize that ice-out is upon us.

Winter still keeps its grip upon the land, although the sun, when it does shine, now hews away at the edges of the snowbanks. The river only grudgingly gives up its ice in a few spots but otherwise remains hard-covered. However I am sure it would be treacherous to walk out on it.

The rock rapids in Fargo, where the spillway used to be, showed a few days ago. Today the rocks are invisible, and the water flows serenely over them, as the river begins to bloat.

Here where I sit, however, a mile south of the rapids, the ice still caps the river, as if winter were taking its time in departing. I only have the feeling, without evidence, that the river is ready to burst its bounds.

There must be an ice-out moment for this stretch of the river. But I expect I would have to wait here patiently, like these tree sentinels, even through the night, to hear the cap crack and witness the moment.

I remember one time, quite a few years back about this time of year, when I attended a meeting one evening near the river. When the meeting was over I went outside and discovered it was a beautiful evening and decided I would walk home "as the crow flies," as they say, from that place on the Moorhead side to my home on the Fargo side a bit farther south. I was carrying a few books under each arm from the meeting.

Now one has to realize that the Red River zig-zags back and forth as it passes between the two cities. So "crossing the river" in the dark as the crow flies means crossing and recrossing it several times. I was not sure from time to time if I was in Minnesota or North Dakota.

Well, it was spring and the ice was soft in places; and at one point, I dropped through the ice. It wasn't very deep; only up to my waist or so. I didn't even get my books wet.

I was more disgusted than anything at my incautious use of the river ice at that time of year. I clambered up onto the ice, walked up to a nearby house and hailed a car from home to come and get me. Spring comes up from underneath on the river.

The ubiquitous crows set up a fuss across the river, probably nagging some predator hawk or owl that has ventured too close to them for their comfort. The bright sun begins to warm the air that was chilled by the night. The day is upon us.

****

At Home in the Woodlands

Back by the Red River once more, I find that the river now gives no evidence of being frozen over.

The first of everything for spring breaks forth today. It's rather exciting and a world of difference from a week ago, when I sat bundled up in this chair and watched the woodchuck (groundhog) trek across the snow on the far side of the river and considered walking across the ice to examine his tracks. Today I would have to swim across. Even the few remaining ice floes are thin and waif-like, and look as if they'll be gone shortly.

When I came here today, although I was aware of the open river and the near-80 degree temperature, I expected only brown surroundings for another week. But a low-hanging branch on the giant American elm near me made me do a double-take, and I went over to take a closer look at it.

I was able to pull a few twigs close to me and, sure enough, the first green of the buds were cracking the brown hulls and beginning to appear. There is no turning back now. New life is advancing and will overtake the winter sleep. At this writing, winter has only three days left before the equinox announces the entrance of spring.

A black butterfly flits by and disappears behind me too quickly for me to identify him. And now a black horse fly lands and checks me out, although he did visit me already last week when snow still lay about me on the ground. A small bird flies into the branches of the big elm, and then moves on. But it appears it was only a chickadee, not a migrant.

Now a real treat! I hear singing in a small oak a short distance away. The light is behind him, so I am at a disadvantage, but I spot his red breast, and I'm delighted to think that I may be seeing my first robin of the season.

He looks like a thrush, but the short chee-ur of his singing is not like the lengthy melody of the robin. I finally work my way around him and spot his blue back and discover, to my equal delight, that I am looking at a bluebird singing his spring song, calling for a mate. I do not call him my first bluebird of the season, for I rarely see a bluebird at all. But the bird guides tell me that he will arrive with the robins, so he is the advance agent of the thrushes this spring.

A pair of wood ducks flashes onto the water directly across the river from me near some old stalks of underbrush. I've learned from before that I need to spot the last place that I've seen them with my naked eye and carefully identify the particular stalks and branches beside them, or else I am hopelessly lost when I try to train my glasses on them, because both waterfowl and upland game birds are such experts at concealment.

After a few moments I pick out the pair, but only because the male flutters a bit, and I am able to trace the colorful outline of his markings. She is even more indistinguishable from her surrounding, nature's way of protecting the nesting female from discovery.

Well! Birdland gave me a show this morning. I doubt that I will often see such a spectacle.

I was scanning the river with my binoculars, as is my habit when I first arrive, when I heard three noisy crows approach a big old dead cottonwood about 50 yards in front of me. I thought, "Ho hum, a couple of crows chasing away a predator," — an event I often hear but almost never see up close.

Suddenly a great horned owl flashed into view and landed in the old cottonwood in front of me. The crows dove at him and hounded him, keeping up their incessant ruckus. Soon other crows joined them, and the ruckus became bedlam.

The owl sat up stiff and straight, with all the dignity he could muster, as if to say, "Oh, these pesky insects; if only someone would shoo them away!" He stared ahead, attempting to ignore them.

They dove at him, and although the great-horned owl is two feet tall, the crow is a considerable bird in itself. Some of the dive-bombers actually hit him about the head. He just puffed up his white collar a bit, adjusted his balance and proceeded to ignore them some more.

It is interesting that crows will take on this king of the treetops, for this owl, when slightly wounded, is known to be a fierce antagonist. This upped my impression of the lowly crow.

Finally they drove him off. With only a slight whoosh of his great wings against the air, he almost silently flew off to my right with more than 15 crows in hot pursuit. They were obviously the self-appointed guardians of the woods. Owls have obviously gained a reputation for attacking and hacking to pieces smaller creatures.

Birders tell me we should be seeing warblers and kinglets by these first weeks in April, but they are apparently standing by to the south, waiting for the weather to change. The first Canada geese appear on their northward trek. Yet even they seem to mill around, as if waiting for things to change up north. It is a strange year.

A gray squirrel comes near about 15 feet to my left. Small patches of grass have begun to appear here and there from the work of the infrequent sun, and he seems to have found something in one of them to interest him. The quest for food seems to be a constant activity among the woodland creatures; except for crows, of course, who find time for chasing crooks.

Now there's a sight. A kestrel glides into the wind on the edge of an open area as I am arriving this morning. He flashes his identifying dull orange back in the morning light.

I am perhaps 60 yards away but he doesn't seem disturbed by my presence. I am facing into the wind also, so he is gliding slowly away from me.

He is an amazing aerialist. He seems to hang motionless for a time on the wings of the wind. He lands on a small limb for a moment, then takes off again and hovers some more into the wind. He lands, and then takes flight.

What is he doing? I expect he is hunting for breakfast among the open patches between snow cover. What keen eyes he must have to view game from that distance above the ground.

However he gives me no chance to view him at lunch. After another moment, he veers off to my left and disappears over a small hillock.

******

The river broke out of its bounds last night — a world of difference lies before me this morning. Last evening we went up on the dike to look at the river, and it lay within its banks yet. This morning the banks have disappeared under the rising river.

A pair of mallards patrols the river, flying by me about 30 feet above the water, heading west and then returning to head east. Half a dozen flocks of Canada geese have passed overhead in the past half hour, heading north and ranging in number from 16 to 34. A flock of slate-colored juncos fuss about on the ground in front of me, and a nuthatch scouts a tree trunk. It's as if the woods have come alive with the rising water.

I'm curious to know whether the river rises with the hour. I've placed a marker at its present level. We'll see.

The casing of ice still floats on its winter position, unbroken, with the river spreading out from underneath it through the trees. It occurs to me that the whole sheet of ice floats at least two feet higher this morning than it did last evening. What a massive amount of energy is represented in lifting that load two feet into the air.

I sit 10 feet from the river's edge at the moment, with a forest of ash and elm in front of me with their feet in the water and with the main span of the river beyond that.

It's amazing how quickly the river has changed. One day this past week, the ice covering floated intact on top of the river. The next morning that covering had totally broken up and, in fact, most of the ice floes had already disappeared down river. Today none remain, only an expanse of open water. Its 55-yard width has expanded to perhaps 150 yards at this point on its course. Snow still decorates the edges of the river here and there.

If a gallon of water is represented in a cubic foot or so, what a massive amount of water added to the river stretches before me, 500 cubic feet or so to the opposite bank, just in this small section of the river. That's life-giving water.

I remember viewing a history program on television that described how, at a certain period in earth's history, water rained upon the earth for a million years (the time boggles the mind) until the earth became a water world, with only points of land visible. The massive ebb and flow of water so much command our planet.

I also recall that when we lived in Warwick, N.D., near Devil's Lake, we could drive from Warwick to Devil's Lake and not see the lake. They told of a massive lake that existed a century or so before with a steamboat called the "Minne H." that plied the distance from Minnewaukon to Devil's Lake. It seemed like a fairy tale.

Yet today, that massive lake has returned, we are threatened with losing Minnewaukon, and the lake is only three or four feet from overflowing its banks, spilling into the Sheyenne River basin and threatening many towns and cities in eastern North Dakota. We wonder where all the water comes from. We will continue to watch the rising river for another day or so.

The other evening, some old-timers remarked that they could remember the day when this Red River was so near being dry that you could walk across it and hardly get your shoes wet. Such change.

Ah, beautiful. My pair of mallards is swimming by, not 20 feet in front of me. I check my marker. The river has risen a full inch in the last hour. Spring is upon us.

Everything in nature is budding now. The difference from a week ago, when I could see only the beginning traces of some buds breaking out, is remarkable.

These are the weeks of the flowering of the trees, a period that I have not looked at closely before. The American elms and the prairie willows are in full bloom. The green ash and the white oak are only budding yet, and have not begun to bloom.

On the elm, the bud and the flower are separate — almost together, but still distinctly separate. The bloom, I assume, will form the seed and break off and fall to the ground to begin a new generation — when? In a week or so? Pollination to create the seed will be invisible to us, I expect.

Most people, including myself, have hardly thought that trees flower. Flower? Where's the flower, we might well ask.

Admittedly the elm or willow would hardly be able to win a beauty contest vying with the tulip or daffodil. And regarding the willows, I would agree with that. But the elm is a rather lovely contestant — small and unobtrusive I admit, but lovely in her own way, pushing out long stamen that hang like a pink and green veil from the blossom; each strand ending with a brown anther as tiny as the head of my pencil lead.

I count six of these lovely strands coming out of one blossom, and six out of another. Are they consistent or are they random in their number?

The willow blossom will not do as well in the beauty contest, if I am to be the judge. His protrusion out of the blossom is a banana-shaped ear that reminds me of an ear of corn that is green, and which, I think, will likely remain a mystery to me.

Silky white strands feather the entire surface, amounting to 250 or more on each of the willow "ears," and again, each of which extends down into the ear of corn to fertilize a kernel. Is there, perhaps, not one seed here, but hundreds of seeds? I shall have to be satisfied for today just with the mystery and the marvel of it.

Ma and Pa wood duck have floated out onto the river, and then back in again to their brush haven. They conceal themselves, so I must leave them to whatever sport they happen to be enjoying.

I asked at the Audubon meeting the other night what others are seeing at their feeders. They said purple and house finches, goldfinches, robins and winter birds; no warblers yet.

At Home in the Woodlands

A red squirrel prances around among the dry leaves about 30 yards in front of me, seeking some tidbits to eat, I expect. What does he find at the end of a long, cold winter, if he has exhausted what he stored last fall? Seeds on trees and underbrush, I expect.

The experts tell us we should be seeing red-winged blackbirds, grackles and finches by this time in the spring. The finches have returned, and they are a welcome sight to see after a long winter. They are our early spring visitors.

Six white-tailed deer pass silently about 50 yards behind me, and I catch sight of them out of the corner of my eye, trying hard not to move and disturb them. They are moving toward the denser refuge of the woods along the Red River.

Several pause to gaze in my direction and check me out. One yearling even takes a few curiosity-seeking steps in my direction, watches me for a moment, then turns back to join the group.

They had settled down on the highland for a bit this morning to take in the warmth of the sun. But now that human busyness and noise is about, they prefer the dense river bottom.

A flock of several dozen chickadees settles into some bushes near me. They fuss about, and then all take off together.

A big crow sails in and settles onto an open patch of grass amid the still-pervasive snow to my left, about 15 feet. He seems to have something of interest on the ground that might make breakfast. He eyes me a bit, then seems to accept me and goes about his business.

An even bigger wild turkey heads over to check out what the crow has found. He is a little cautious about me but decides to accept me guardedly and heads for the grass patch and the crow.

Now the question: who will dominate the grass patch? Naturally it would seem to me the smaller crow would give way to the larger turkey. But the crow looks at the turkey, stands his ground and goes back to checking out the grass patch.

After a few minutes, the turkey departs. A moment later, a juvenile gray squirrel appears and heads for the grass patch. Now I surmise that the larger crow will intimidate the small squirrel. Not so.

A squirrel moves in like he owns the place and doesn't even bother to expend a glance in the crow's direction. Crow gives way to squirrel and flies off. It's as if a pecking order is programmed into these woodland creatures.

****

The river has crested this morning. I am looking out at the highest level the Red River will reach this year, between 39 and 40 feet, before it begins to recede.

It spreads out now like a sprawling giant upon the land, stretching half a mile across to the Minnesota side, saying, in effect, "This is my river land. I only lend it to you for some months each year, when I retreat to my quiet river bottom."

A giant clay dike greeted me this morning at the spot where I sat last week. The river presses perhaps four feet up the

At Home in the Woodlands

dike on the water side. The dike itself reaches four feet up into the air.

Good old Red River Valley gumbo. We curse it sometimes when we try to cultivate it. But today we bless it as a stout, solid barricade for our protection against the advancing river. It will hold well against the rising tide, until the river recedes and the workmen return to shovel it up and carry it away again. A light mist hangs in the air this morning. If one stepped on the gumbo, it would stick to one's shoes like glue.

Of course, the geese and the ducks are having a heyday. They seem to think this big puddle is made just for them as they pass through on their great migration. I hear them honking on all sides.

Four days ago we drove by the Arrowhead Waterfowl Refuge in north central North Dakota on the great flyway that passes down from Manitoba through the Dakotas and Nebraska. The sight that greeted our eyes made us pull over and just gaze in amazement at the spectacle and listen to the cacophony of sound.

The snow geese were passing over and just wheeling around in the air over the area. It was late in the afternoon, and they were looking for some open water (much of it was frozen yet) or fields where they could rest for the night. We estimated 8-9,000 geese at that time, circling in the air above us.

When we first saw them on the horizon, they looked like swarms of mosquitoes. But when we opened our car windows and listened, there was no mistaking what they were. Also at first they seemed to be entirely snow geese. But as they landed on the fields near us, we could see some were Canada geese.

A few have landed on the Red River flood now and paddle about among the tall trees sticking out of the water. Robins serenade us everywhere in the mornings now with the songs of spring. Our son in Los Angeles tells us they have no robins there, and he enjoyed being reminded of them.

Meanwhile, the river giant moves lazily by us as it travels on to the north.

The images of nature that repeat themselves tend to be precious to us humans who are mostly rooted in one spot on the planet, while the world changes around us. It is precious to us to know that the robin will come again and that the geese will greet us once again, as they fly overhead on their tireless repetition of migration back north in the spring. It would be very disappointing to us if either one of those phenomena failed to happen some spring.

Three white-tailed deer have just gone dancing past to my left. They came up from behind so I didn't notice them until they were alongside. They must have discovered me just then, and it spooked them. They broke into a run but in no great alarm, and they've stopped ahead to gaze back at me. As I seem to pose no threat, they walk on, browsing at their evening supper.

******

This spring morning I find myself back in the quiet little cemetery in the center of Minnetonka that I visited two months ago in the dead of winter. The view looks down on a charming little park with table, shelter, duck pond and all — one of those best-kept secrets found in the center of many Minnesota towns, which any traveler could find if he took the trouble to inquire at the first gas station he encountered as he entered the town.

(I've always wondered how the gas station has become the repository of all knowledge across America.)

A chill still greets me when I come out in the morning, but in warmer weather I would love to sit at that table and write someday. However what also greets me as I come out in the morning now is a serenade of songbirds. It is as if nature, robed in snow just weeks ago, has suddenly shed her winter garments and dances forth in the gaiety of new life.

A cardinal delights me with his whistle. I see him and whistle back. He responds but is too timid to let me come much closer, or perhaps too busy with singing in a spring mate to be bothered with this oversized pretend cardinal who was whistling at him. At any rate, he entertains me with his flash of red as he flits among the trees.

Here at the cemetery a songbird sings to me with his trill, followed by a series of three descending trills. But he sits high in the upper terraces of a tall maple with his back maddeningly to the light so that I can only make out the outline of a small bird with the binoculars. You who are more adept at bird songs than I would be able to tell me immediately what I am seeing.

A crow is being chased by a small bird — a kingbird? — through a grove of white pines, the latter suggesting subtly that the big fellow is not welcome in the neighborhood.

I'm always impressed with how tolerant birds are of us humans. It's almost as if they've long ago learned that we're stuck to the earth and not about to fly up among the branches to bother them.

The peregrine falcon, for example, which has recently returned to its downtown nesting box among the tall buildings in Fargo, abides our presence remarkably well. He is a lesson in tolerance.

When the banders come in and take the four chicks out for an hour to band them, he gets royally upset; but he doesn't abandon the nest, nor does he abandon the chicks when we return them to his nest. We can even move his nesting box and chicks to another high building (for some inscrutable human reason) and he follows the box and continues his care. Amazing.

Now two crows nearby set up a ruckus as if a predator were in the area and, sure enough, a Cooper's hawk sails into view above the still winter-appearing ash trees 100 yards in front of me. He soars about in a lordly fashion, and then disappears to my right.

The Cooper is an amazing aerialist. Up high he seems to drift effortlessly on the drafts of air. On other occasions I have seen him zip by at eye level, not 15 feet in front of me like a rocket, intent upon some chase after a hapless victim. On that occasion he rounded some brush cover right beside me on his chase, or else I am sure he would not have flown that close to me.

A gray squirrel bobs in and out of the grass patch to my left. He is a restless creature compared to the calm turkey. Squirrel bobs off to a nearby stump for a few minutes and preens himself. Then he returns to nosing about in the grass for a leisurely breakfast.

****

The high water of the Red River is goose heaven. A few small flocks sail low above the open water in front of me but don't land. Birder opinions still waver as to whether we are seeing any migrating geese yet or seeing a stirring among the locals that have wintered here by the city lagoon. The Christmas bird count tabulated 9,000 Canada geese that wintered here this year. In spite of an exceptionally long season of cold this winter, the temperatures have not been especially low. The slow thaw this spring has been a blessing for tempering the flooding. The city is well ready with temporary clay dikes at vulnerable places and hundreds of pallets of sandbags at the ready for a flood surge.

Mid-May is supposed to be the time of the optimum migration of songbirds through the area, and that is only two weeks away. I hope they do not get too cold a welcome.

I asked the Audubon folks what happens if birds arrive too soon and it turns very cold on them. They tell me that some of them die. But they say that some species have an incredible facility for sensing the temperatures and stay south until it is time to move north.

*****

The river has allowed me to come over the dike and sit by the rivershore again this morning for the first time since the flood. I say "rivershore" advisedly, because the line of willows that marks the bank of the summer river is still 80 yards ahead of me over a span of fast-moving water.

A pair of flickers romps among some saplings to the left of me, and another one probes for his breakfast on the ground to my right. A pair of small teal swims by in front of me, and now another pair joins them. All of this pairing up! It must be true that in spring, a young male's fancy ... A pair of robins has already built a nest in the corner of our porch.

The giant earthmovers have started to remove the temporary gumbo dikes further south along the river that were needed to protect the city from flood waters. Being unacquainted with the verbiage in these parts, a foreigner from St. Paul asked me the other day what gumbo is. (I know — it sounds like an Alabama soup of some kind.) It is the heavy, thick bed of clay that underlies the rich, black topsoil in the Red River Valley.

The big spreading elm tree with the four foot diameter trunk has a jump on some of the others and is starting to sport miniature one-inch leaves. I will love to sit under that tree in a few weeks, when the ground around it is not so spongy from the flood. I am gradually chasing the river back to where it belongs. In another 30 feet, it will be back below its banks again.

That heavy bed of clay, of course, is what keeps Leech Lake or any of the other great Minnesota lakes from seeping away into the soil. It hadn't occurred to me before, but this same bed of clay here is what kept and held up that mega-giant, Lake Agassiz, for thousands of years before we came along.

A stretch of the bike path lies about three feet behind me now. I didn't expect any traffic today, because the path disappears into the water 100 yards in either direction from me. But my good neighbor, Rick Rotzien, who loves the riverfront, came over to the dike and found the path and me a few minutes ago. However, Rick is a mine of information about the riverfront, so it is a pleasure to visit with him in this setting. He pointed out a great horned owl nest, an active one, across the river on the Minnesota side, 250 yards in front of me. He also pointed out a habitat across the river where he often sees turkey vultures in the summer.

We saw a good view of a fox sparrow, poking about among some dry leaves, flashing his reddish tail at us. And my John B. Grant — "Our Common Birds" — reports that by late April, most of the fox sparrows have passed on north.

I should add a note for those who are wondering who this John B. Grant is to whom I frequently refer, when I should be carrying about my Roger Tory Peterson, like a good twitcher would. Grant is one of those old-looking books that would look right at home alongside McGuffey's Reader. The full title of his book is "Our Common Birds and How to Know Them." It was published by Charles Scribner's Sons in New York in 1891; but of course, birds don't change all that much in 120 years. His illustrations are black and white photo shots of taxidermy birds. Primitive, yes, but he is skilled in helping you to know and love birding.

Will you look at that! One male mallard is chasing the devil out of another one, splashing about on the surface of the river in front of me. And to the right of them with my binoculars, I spot the cause of it all, a hen, waiting for them to settle the argument. Ah, this pairing is sometimes a rocky road.

****

I'm back for the first time this year to the spot where I wrote last summer, in the woods near Ham Lake. I'm still bundled to the hilt in jackets and such, but the air is warm enough for me to operate with bare hands.

While I've been gone, the local mammal residents have visited the small spot in the brush I had tramped down, leaving their signature scat — deer and bear. It's midday now, and they are no doubt resting in the deep brush in the warmth of the May sun, away from a chilling north breeze that still cools the land. Robins serenade me on either side, as well as the towhee with his familiar "chewink," whom I spot directly ahead of me.

A loon greeted me on the lake when I came out this morning, and it is good to hear him. He's back to herald the new summer season. Some migrating geese honked as they passed overhead on their way north.

A song sparrow, with the smart black spot on his vest, nods at me from a nearby branch, but he doesn't favor me with a song. It seems that mating season is mostly past, and nesting season is upon us. I have seen robins, with newly-made nests, sitting on their eggs already.

This is a good time to see migrating birds. I notice the ornithologists list dozens of species arriving now — catbirds, swallows, thrushes, warblers, vireos and many others. Still, the cool lingers in the air, and I have to warm my hands from time to time. The small oaks near me have not even started to show buds. The ubiquitous alder, however, is sporting small buds and pushing the season.

The woods are so transparent now, enabling one to see far into them without any foliage covering the view. We wish for warmer days to set things budding and blooming. We have seen the pasque flower (crocus) and scilla in bloom. I guess we'll just have to let nature come when it will.

The stately Norway pines rise 80 feet into the air in front of me. I hear the low soughing of the wind through their upper branches. It is a peaceful sound. The birch and oaks around them sway with them in the winds, as they await their time of foliage.

When we lived in the Yukon, the trees were remarkable to me. Down south here, I had always felt getting to know the trees was an insurmountable task. We have perhaps 150 or more species. The Yukon, however, has only 10 species, a number one could easily get one's mind around. That made tree studies fun. The further north you go, the fewer the tree species. Only the hardy survive. The last to go in the far, far north is the black spruce.

A wood pewee nods at me from a nearby branch. He'd like an insect or two on the wing, but there are mighty few of such insects here yet.

Everything seems quiet here at Ham Lake with the woods seemingly still. Only the soughing of the wind off the lake in the tall Norways disturbs the quiet.

Then a crow with his cawing sails overhead to remind me that he is still around. Then a second joins him, and they disappear over the tree line to the north.

And now I discover the hackberrry, just 10 inches in front of me, is pushing its green buds out, breaking the brown husks that surround them. The oaks, alder and birch are slower to begin, but the hackberry buds are a signal that the others will follow soon. No doubt out of the deep woods, where the sun better warms the world, life is ahead of us here.

A wild turkey breaks out of the woods from my right as I walk down the trail, going in the direction I am going. I keep moving ahead slowly, and he keeps moving ahead of me at a hearty trot, seemingly in no hurry to take flight.

The trail goes straight ahead for some distance, so I am able to watch his progress for quite a while. I am amazed at his foot speed. I doubt I could catch him on a dead run. Then he disappears around a bend in the road.

Now a robin appears, landing in the top of a young white oak to the left of me. He offers no song. Is his mating over, and he's into nest building now? A common tern greets me over the lake behind me.

A gray squirrel moves into view on the ground straight ahead of me about 30 yards. I train the glasses on him and he promptly haps behind a small tree.

At Home in the Woodlands

I wait for him to come out the other side. He seems to be just ambling along the forest floor, so I expect him to reappear, but he fools me. I am still looking. Did he walk straight away from me behind the cover of the tree, or did he climb the far side of the tree? Did I hear the scratching of claws on bark? Does he have a home up that tree?

The weatherman promised a rainy, miserable day today, and I'm afraid the weather has made a liar out of him. It's cool, but the sun is bright and it's anything but miserable.

I'm looking to see if I can see any evidence of green on the forest floor, but I see none. The six-inch, two-cluster Norway pine needles make a thick bed on the ground around me. Burrowing my finger down through them, I find they form a bed two inches deep before I reach something that might be called soil.

Pressing my hand on top of them I find them springy to the touch. I am thinking it would not be uncomfortable to sleep on the bare ground here, and bare ground is normally too hard for my old bones to afford me a good night's sleep.

A crow visits me off to my right again, calling to a companion. Now he is quiet. Evening is here. It is time for him to settle in.

****

The American elm has produced an exquisite little leaf 1.5 inches long, the perfect suggestion of what its full-grown leaf will look like in a few weeks. Its flower seems to have mostly dropped away.

The green ash has produced a 1.5-inch leaf as well, and the red maple, not to be outdone, has put forth a lovely red 2-inch leaf. The erstwhile leaves of summer are beautiful to see in miniature.

Now suddenly the big American elm ahead of me has become alive with small birds, as if on command. The common yellowthroat comes down to the ground for a few minutes to give me a good look with his bold white wing bars. He is joined by two others and then they take off up into the big elm again. All through the tree are myrtle warblers as well, with splashes of yellow on their sides and rumps.

The ubiquitous nuthatch toodles up and down the tree trunk to join in the gala parade. A light rain sets in; and now, as suddenly as they appeared, they are all gone, leaving the big elm empty once more.

It occurs to me I can thank the tiny leaves for giving me this good view of the flock of visitors. In mid-summer full foliage would not allow nearly as good a show. Of course by mid-May these warblers would have resumed their migration northward, so I wouldn't see them anyway. This is good warbler season. To where do the non-nesting birds retire in heavy downpours? Someone must know. Perhaps there are a thousand refuges in these giant trees, if we could know them.

Gray squirrel ambles about on the grass in search of food. He doesn't seem to mind the rain. We've had an inch in the last few days, sort of half attempts to water the earth. We should get another inch today; a real April shower.

The Red River in front of me doesn't seem to mind these casual wettings. It just takes in what comes and rolls on in its ancient way.

A bufflehead duck lands on the river in front of me. He paddles lazily about, in no great hurry to get anywhere. A pair of teal flies by going south. Two mallards do the same going north.

Before spotting the waterfowl, I was sitting and bemoaning the fact that no bird life entertained me as I sat in my old riverside haunt for the first time this year, since the river went down below its banks again after the flood.

Then, as if on command, a beautiful myrtle warbler with his white breast and yellow rump, flew into the dry weed stalks 20 feet in front of me and gave me plenty of time to get a good look at him

Following the warbler, a chipping sparrow with his rusty cap and faint yellowish markings flew into the same spot and began feeding. Then two green-winged teal sailed in and landed gently on the river in front of me. Then two cowbirds settled into the leafless ash tree nearby. So the bird parade has indeed begun.

Now the grasshopper sparrow visits to my left, a tiny fellow with a yellow breast and striped cap. He bobs about among the short dry grasses, searching and feeding and finally flies off.

The buds on the trees have just begun to burst open, in most cases not even suggesting the outline of new leaves, except on the willows. A clear blue cloudless sky greets me, but the air remains cool. The temperature last night dropped below freezing. Winter is only grudgingly giving way to spring and here it is, the opening of fishing season.

Yet young love buds in spite of a slow spring. Birds are appearing in couples, as I've mentioned above, promising new life.

The river receded quickly below its banks, and the rainless weather has dried up the riparian area immediately so I can walk to within a few yards of the river bank before hitting any muddy remains of the flood. The old grasses and weeds are silted down with the dirt residue. Although it makes things look a bit untidy by Good Housekeeping standards, I am reminded of how the Egyptians blessed the flooding of the Nile for the rich soil nourishment it laid down on their fields.

The little grasshopper sparrows come surprisingly close to me for their ground feeding. They do not seem to mind me as long as I do not move quickly.

I observe the little ash tree about 30 feet to my left that I watched in its young growth during last year's season of no floods. I was curious whether it would live to grow another year, since no trees, that is, seedlings, survive in this riparian area. Only the old established trees go on.

The young ash stands five feet tall now. It was covered by the flood this spring. It is slow to bud out, but it seems to be otherwise none the worse for wear and was not broken by ice floes or drifting debris that lies scattered around. Was it just lucky?

Even the few big surviving trees had to begin as saplings many decades ago. How remarkable is the flow of life.

A short period of time produces a world of difference upon the river front. The river is now an open, flowing stream without a sign of ice anymore. Some warm days have accomplished this.

The air is cold this morning, however — 30 degrees. I have to keep warming my fingers. The land is still dormant, awaiting some real warming days to come to life.

Bird life, however, is another matter. For them, the open water is enough to signal spring.

Three Canada geese fly overhead as I am coming here this morning. They are headed north. A green-winged teal skims by, 50 feet in front of me, just above the surface of the river.

A sharp-shinned hawk raises a fuss to my right across the river, and then rises into view and leisurely skims the tops of the oak and ash trees, passing across my line of vision on the other side of the river, revealing his white-streaked breast, which I can easily pick up in my glasses. He passes to my left and disappears behind the trees.

I go down to the river bank and surprise four mallards who quickly fly off. I scold myself that I didn't approach more carefully.

I spot another pair at some distance to my right. Now two mallards fly in and settle into the water across from me. Two more teal pass overhead. Now another pair of mallards flies by.

I had remarked earlier that I had not seen any waterfowl here for the past two seasons and wondered why that was. I mentioned this to my Audubon friends, but they assured me this lack of birds must have been the case for the stretch of river I was watching, for waterfowl were, indeed, around elsewhere.

The return of waterfowl to this place is a welcome sight. They really herald the coming of spring. And now, to endorse that idea, another pair of mallards flies leisurely by, not 30 feet in front of me. The parade of birds doesn't end.

Of course there must be meaning in the speed of birds in flight, but sometimes that speed puzzles me. Why does it vary?

An hour ago I saw a pair of mallards fly, hell bent for leather. No one was chasing them. No gunshots frightened them. I couldn't imagine a destination that beckoned them on at that breakneck speed.

Then 10 minutes ago, I saw a pair fly by like they were on a Sunday afternoon stroll, climbing and dipping in a most disorderly manner. Now what sense does one make out of flight like that.

And now it is a slate-colored junco that perches near me. In any event, I am grateful today for the bird parade.

The woods are alive with sound. It's a joy just to stand still and listen to the many sounds. A dove sings its mournful song across the river. A robin sings out heartily behind me.

At Home in the Woodlands

Earlier I had seen the goldfinch sporting about among the low branches of a green ash tree. A white-crowned sparrow busied himself scratching about among the dry leaves on the ground in search of some lunch. The purple finch, with its upper body brightly colored in its purple-red, hopped about in nearby bushes.

My migration guide tells me that I can look for white-throated sparrows, towhees, brown thrashers and house wrens to appear now at the end of April. Winter wrens and fox sparrows will have passed on north.

The forest floor is beginning to green up all around me. The brome grass is flourishing and the young plantains are beginning to show. Even a small purple violet blooms on a nearby hillside. Gradually spring arrives amidst cool weather.

And now a special treat presents itself to me. A Philadelphia vireo capers about among the old dry aster stalks to the right about 40 feet away. He lingers a good while, giving me a fine chance to examine his 5.25-inch frame in my binoculars. I am able to see clearly his unbarred wings and the faint tinge of yellow on his upper breast. Peterson's guide tells me he breeds in northern North Dakota, so he is right on schedule.

He started in the lower branches of a green ash tree and then flew down to the 4-foot aster stalks. He took his time flitting from stalk to stalk, hanging nimbly on the sturdy stalk.

Now he is joined by two song sparrows who are doing the same balancing act on the aster stalks. What is it that they are finding? Some of these stalks are a few inches from my chair. I pull off one of the dried blossoms, the same blossoms that graced my sitting here eight months ago, and indeed I find a hard seed at the base of each blossom. This area of apparently old, dried, useless stalks provides plenty of food for these seed-eaters.

A flicker descends from a young white oak tree to my left and promenades on some open space on the forest floor. I had heard a wick-wick-wick sound across the river earlier but couldn't see the singer. It must have been he. A wood duck paddles by. The woods are alive with life again.

****

I find myself in a maple forest today near Minnetonka. Several small birds, perhaps vireos, visit to the right of me, but they depart too quickly to identify for sure. Hopefully they will return. Meanwhile the midafternoon quiet settles upon the forest.

I am completely surrounded by silver maple. There seems to be no exception to this species as far as the eye can see. Somehow it has dominated the land in this place.

It does afford me a good opportunity to take a close look at this tree, a chance the woods do not often give. They present themselves as stately giants, beautiful to behold. Although the maple does not spread like the elm, it makes a thick canopy, leaving the floor of the forest almost free of brush. Only a space at the base of the steep hill where I sit is open and covered with dense brush. The space is surrounded by hills on all sides, making it a natural catch basin for water run-off.

The beautiful maple leaves on this tree grow differently up the twig than the elm, ash or oak. They stretch out on their stems only off the end of each twig and seem invariably to grow four to a cluster. The stem is rounded, not flat like the aspen, and yet the configuration on the twig seems to make a forest of them tremble in the lightest breeze.

A maple denizen of the woods towers 65 feet in the air directly in front of me. Two black crows sail silently into its branches and rest there. A third one sails in from my right. One sets up a cawing but now is silent. It does not seem to be a caw of alarm. He seems to be only calling in the others. Although they still rest nearby, they seem to be only passing through.

The giant maple I mentioned seems to have progeny all around. Some are only eight inches in girth. The lord maple himself stretches out over 6.5 feet in circumference at the base of the trunk.

Two Canada geese fly over, headed for Lake Minnetonka, barely visible through the trees. I am led to wonder if I would be able to identify this tree by its bark in the dead of winter when I do not have the advantage of these impressive leaves. The smaller maples only 15 inches or so in circumference look very much like white ash, and I am afraid they would confuse me. The lord maples, however, have the flaky bark that is similar to the red maple. We shall see if I remember that. The forest floor, of course, is carpeted by brown maple leaves. It is amazing to think that millions of leaves above will fall in six months to make a new carpet. A cardinal and robin call from out of sight behind me, and a woodpecker hammers away to my left. But I must be content to be without the return of the vireos.

*****

Back at the Red River, I catch sight of the ever-busy beaver going about his work upriver from me about 100 yards. He slips into cover under the river bank, so I go upriver to get a better look.

I find evidence of a half-made house; not much more than a pile of work half-done, with his evident tooth marks at the ends of the sticks. It is old work. It doesn't appear he's added to it. He's apparently back, revisiting the project.

I stand next to the project, scanning the river to see if I can spot him surface. As I turn away for a moment, would you know, he surfaces behind me, discovers me, slaps the water and dives again. All he leaves for me to see is the ring on the water.

A song sparrow serenades me to my left. I come closer and finally discover him, perched with amazing agility on the top of a new 5-foot willow stalk by the river's edge.

He doesn't seem much disturbed by my presence, just intent upon serenading whoever around here might want to listen; perhaps a prospective mate? He fills the air with his three note tseet-tseet-tseet, followed by a melodious six-note trill.

He turns about on his perch so that I am able to study his light-streaked breast with his distinctive black "stickpin" at the center of the vest. He is definitely one of the joys of spring.

At Home in the Woodlands

Suddenly three noisy Canada geese come tearing clamorously down the river across my line of vision, flying about five feet above the surface of the water. They seem intent on racing each other toward some distant destination. For all their noise, they are a magnificent sight.

A pair of mallards settles onto the river across from me and swims about. It is good to see so many waterfowl on this stretch of the river again. I sometimes wonder what kind of food a moving river offers for waterfowl. I'm sure a still pond offers more. Perhaps open water is just a safe, pleasurable place for them to spend some time. At least they give me pleasure.

I look to see more signs of sprouting as the weather warms, but it is slow to come. Some first shoots of grass appear under foot. The trees all seem to be waiting yet for a little more warmth. A few bushes, like the lilacs, have just begun to shoot out their buds; they are the advance guard.

The warmth of the spring sun is pleasant as I sit here, however. It is a world of difference from a week ago when my fingers kept getting numb from the cold, and I had to stop and warm them.

Finally the heavens have opened and let loose the spring rains upon the earth, after a long, cool, arid spring. Things are a bit wet and soppy, but we do not begrudge the good earth this welcome drink.

Now the great "grass-washing" has happened. It is as if a disguising cloak has marked each blade of grass and suddenly, in an afternoon, in an hour, even, the downpour has thrown off the disguising mask and there stands, revealed, the green, green grass of spring in all of its emerald beauty. Of course the cloak is not true; it is only a poetic way of mine to try to capture the magic appearance of the first green grass. It is good for the soul.

We are nearing the optimum bird migration time through this area. I recall hearing that mid-May sees the maximum warbler population moving through. Already some of the songbirds have appeared, and it is pleasant to see them.

The late spring rains water the land. Of course no birds brave the pouring rain, but rather they find suitable shelter somewhere. Again I ask: What hiding places do thousands of birds find for themselves in pouring rain? There aren't enough cavities and caves for all of them. Do they simply hunker down and let the rain roll off their water repellent feathers? I must ponder this more.

I am having the pleasant experience of finding myself facing a very bright yellow, lovely bush 50 feet in front of me. My first thought is that it must be covered with old leaves that did not shed themselves last fall. Obviously when I have been here before I have not observed whether or not they were present.

I trundled over to them in the rain and discovered they are not old leaves but are rather gorgeous yellow blossoms — absolutely beautiful blooms. They are a joyous addition to the end-of-winter woods. It is forsythia.

Each blossom has four petals and is 1.5 inches across, and they boast about six blossoms to a twig. The pistils are yellow nodes in the centers and the stamens are nondescript entities around the centers, typical female-male descriptions.

At Home in the Woodlands

The blossoms all face downward. Is this to allow for the stamen-to-pistil fertilization by gravity? But is this not done by insects from a second bush to my left? Ah, it is, indeed, the season of the birds and the bees!

A tom turkey strolls on the far bank of the river to my right. He ambles into the woods, disappears and later appears down on the bank again to my left. He ambles along leisurely, not feeding, just seeming to enjoy a riverside stroll in the warm spring sun.

A pair of mallards sails along; another drake joins them, and he is quickly shooed off downriver to find his own company. I am able to get very close to them behind the concealment of some underbrush, and I am struck by the color on the drake's head in the very bright sun. As he turns, it seems to change to an iridescent blue, then back to green. What a brilliant display of color.

A pair of chickadees has moved into the white ash to my right, then up into the big elm directly above me and not 30 feet away. They lunch busily on elm seeds, not able to eat without chattering at the same time.

The sun has broken out from behind the big white oaks behind me, bathing me in sunlight, which is not unpleasant on this perfect spring day. With the appearance of sunlight, suddenly a shimmering single strand of web comes into view, invisible before and so close I could reach out and touch it. It spans a distance of three feet between two of last year's white aster stalks.

A spider has been busy spinning the web for the last day. It's so fragile I could have walked through it without noticing, yet so tough that it whips in the wind without breaking. How in the world does the spider cast a web across that distance?

It brings to mind that on many mornings over the year, I walked the paths of Templar Point on Leech Lake in the early morning hours. If the sun was just right, shining from behind me, I became aware that I was walking through dozens, perhaps hundreds of very thin webs. I had walked those paths the evening before and broken any existing webs, so these had to have been spun overnight — in the last 12 hours. It made me realize that daily, as I walked through these woods, I must have walked through thousands without knowing it. I must be clothed in webs by the end of the day, without it ever even disturbing me.

A myrtle warbler flits into the big elm. He ignores the ample seed supply and seems to be searching for insects.

I cannot leave the day without noting the lush quack grass that has grown up around me, even over the last week or so, covering the once-bare flat of this riparian area. Its leaves grow out alternately on its stem. I am wondering how and when it flowers and produces seeds. I have certainly much more to learn to know about grasses on our globe, that we utterly depend on and take very much for granted.

A small teal races silently across my line of vision, down the length of the river. Otherwise, bird life seems to have settled down for the close of the day.

Spring is mighty slow in coming to these parts. Here it is, mid-May, and the terrain looks like mid-March.

A house wren greets me about 10 feet to my right, as he hops about after some morsels that interest him on a very small bush. I say "greets me," but he only does this by the sight of him, not with any sound. This is food-gathering time, not wren-singing time. That will come in due time, when he has his nest built and is seeking a mate.

Now that I mention nest building, I realize he is working not in a bush but in a green ash sprout, feathered out in debris from the recently subsided flood of the Red River. It boasts a dandy supply of good nest-making materials. So that may well be what he is doing. Here are some downy fibers for his nest.

Of course, what appears to us as a bit of a mess is actually a blessing to this riparian area. The area prospers from the soaking. It has flooded in and out so quickly that it has killed nothing.

A very short growth of grass appears everywhere, where there was no grass two weeks ago. The river has left a very thin layer of good Red River Valley silt upon the land, a rich addition to the river bank. A small shower quickly washes the silt off the plants and down into the soil, leaving everything looking fresh and green again.

Almost all the trees now have begun to sprout buds. The cottonwoods have already flowered and dropped their flowers to the ground.

I became curious about a young, 6-foot green ash tree, whose progress I've been following for several years now. So I took a trek down to observe it, although that area is a bit muddy yet from the recent flood.

Although that youngster is un-budded as yet, it stands healthy and unbowed, its branches decorated with the feathery adornment of twigs and grasses left by the flood, which won't hurt it at all. That's good.

However around me in the copse of green ash in which I sit at the moment, I see lots of beaver work. I can count from where I sit 17 of these ash that have been cut off and hauled to the river. They range in diameter from one-and-a-half to three inches. The next challenge my young ash faces when it reaches that size is the attack of the river beavers. They have no mercy on those who've shown even the most valiant efforts at survival. Survival in the woods requires a lot of luck.

A monarch butterfly flashes by eight feet in front of me, darting back and forth, giving quite a show, then heading toward the river. Another one joins him.

It is good to see the monarchs again; a welcome sign that summer is near. They had not joined me a week ago, although I did see them during the week. So they have returned in their migration from Mexico for another year.

I am told they depend on milkweed to subsist. So milkweed must be present in this allowed-to-grow riparian area that stretched up 30 yards from the river bank. I have not observed the new growth flora carefully enough to discover them. I expect I'll be able to do it better in autumn when the pods are visible. But the monarchs tell me that milkweed is here.

Speaking of new growth, I remain curious about the appearance of the new growth of the white aster, whose tall brown stalks from last year stand all around. A week ago I couldn't see this new growth. This week I can see it, and perhaps could have last week if I'd looked closely, standing about eight inches tall all around. Although I am not good at identifying their new growth, I would almost wager that is what I am observing. New growth in the forest is thrilling in its own way. It appears not creeping in, like the inchworm, but with a flourish like a thousand sandhill cranes suddenly taking flight. And I suppose I could look at it in the same spot, year after year for a lifetime, and never discover all that it has to offer.

The cottonwood a few hundred yards behind me is dropping seeds and floating bits of fleecy down; not much, just a bit now and then. As I look up, it matches the fleecy cumulous clouds that float lazily southward across the deep blue sky.

Today we enter the last period in the spring bird migration cycle. During the next 10 days, the blackpoll warblers will pass through going north, along with yellow-bellied flycatchers; although I must confess I have yet to see the latter, and it has been 43 years since I have seen the former. Marsh wrens will appear for the summer, and cardinals are coming now to stay. Cardinals have always been around south of us in the summer, but we are seeing more of them in our area the last few years.

The white cabbage butterfly flits about, insisting that I mention it. It has been with us for several weeks, the first of the butterflies to arrive in this area. Those two drakes seem to be insisting on the same notice, for here they go again.

****

A merry red-winged blackbird greets me from the edge of the river as I come in today. And immediately, a rose-breasted grosbeak flies into a white oak tree 20 yards in front of me and poses for a long time to give me a good chance to study him.

Today finds me in an IBA along the Red River. IBA is a designation tossed around by birders that simply means Important Bird Area. It is one of hundreds of such areas across the U.S. set aside for conservation, not to be disturbed by motor vehicles or hunting.

These weeks in May are the optimum time for warbler migration through this area. It is a great time to come out to a place like this and see birds. One birder I spoke to said she had seen and identified 13 birds in a short while. Some are especially exciting to see, like the palm warbler and black and white warbler; the latter, they tell me, characteristically runs up and down tree trunks.

The grosbeak is serenading me with his spring song. He sounds very much like the robin. He has a lovely voice.

Among the birds previously sighted, I don't see the turkey, which surprises me. He has proliferated so much that we are now in the middle of a bow hunting season for that bird. Happily this is a "no hunting" area, but in some areas where I've sat, I wondered if I might see arrows whizzing past.

A female goldfinch lighted in a dogwood bush not six feet to my left. She danced around among the branches, and then flew off. Now a swamp sparrow with its rusty cap and gray breast lights in a green ash tree to my left. He sports about among the branches, giving me a good chance to study him.

The woods are greening up gradually. Open spaces are green now with brome grass. The prairie willows and green ash have begun to leaf out, as has the dogwood near me.

The oaks still stand stark and bare, the last to leaf out and the longest to live. Is there a lesson in that somewhere? They will leaf out in their own time.

The green ash has begun to flower as well as leaf out. The flower can be seen hanging down from the same axis as the leaf. It bears an exquisite flower. A magenta petal hangs down and protects a yellow-green pistil and stamen. Eight such blossoms hang on each flowering stem; at least it is eight on the stem I am observing; it may be more on other stems. I expect they hang down to facilitate reproduction. What insects do they depend on for cross-fertilization; or is it simply wind?

*****

In the North, the warm days of spring meld into summer quite gracefully. On the calendar, we post this moment at the summer solstice on the 21st day of June. But in our skin, we feel it weeks before that.

As a child, I marked it the day our mother let us doff the trousers of winter and don the shorts of summer. That usually happened sometime in May. To us youngsters, that moment suggested a great sense of newness and release. School ended for us youngsters, officially marking the beginning of summer for us, as we looked forward to lots of days out-of-doors. The giant cottonwood at the corner of the open acre behind our home offered welcome shade on hot summer days. The county men came out to remove the long wooden snow fence across the center of that acre, which suddenly expanded our world. We soon inhabited our tree fort again in the tall boxelder at the end of the acre next to the neighbors horse pasture. Summer was upon us.

Now, once again comes the time when summer settles in. Trees end their blossoming, form their seeds, and drop those seeds to the earth to begin a new generation.

Chapter 5: The Birth of a Monarch Butterfly

I spot the bright red of a cardinal in a big basswood tree, as I prepare to sit near a cattail marsh in the woods. I no sooner see him than he entertains me with his beautiful song.

Presently a second cardinal joins him. Of course; it is that season. In a moment, they fly off together.

Soon I hear the warbling song of the red-winged blackbird, out among the cattails, competing with the deep-throated song of the bullfrogs. The red wing flies up from the marsh and lights in a nearly-leafless ash above me.

I study him through my binoculars for a time then decide, since he is so directly overhead, it is not a good spot. It is the better part of valor for me to move on, lest he send down a deposit.

Vestiges of spring linger on the doorstep of summer; it is interesting to what a varying degree the trees have leafed out. Some are ready for summer. The American elm to my left and the big basswoods in front of me are well on their way. The prairie willows and poplars down by the marsh are going full-bore.

Some are slower. The silver maple only has small leaves. The white ash is just getting started. And a couple of young trees behind me are so far behind that they are barely bursting their buds. Without leaves, I am hard pressed to identify them. Are they ironwoods?

The apple trees farther away are in full bloom, of course; they are lovely.

The first spring insects have begun to appear. A white cabbage butterfly flits away among some blossoms. It qualifies as my first butterfly of the season. A small spider graces the sleeve of my jacket. He pauses, preens himself a bit and then scurries off to do whatever spiders do. He seems to be a rather full-bodied fellow.

An even smaller spider scoots across my trouser leg, pausing from time to time before moving on. He seems to have no body at all and appears to be all legs.

To my right I see a tiny white spider beginning his work. He lets me watch him climb up and down the thin filament of his web. He is no bigger than the point of a dull pencil.

Of course, I cannot see his web. It is invisible to the naked eye, or even to the magnification of binoculars. Yet, of course, I say that it is there and I am sure that you would stand by me in this matter.

I can testify to the presence of webs such as his as I walk through the deep woods in the early morning and gather webs across my face as I break through them. Yet I do not see them.

It is a curious thing about us humans as we encounter the deep woods (and perhaps as we encounter anything in life, for that matter), that we feel the necessity to fill in what we do not understand, so that we can move on. It is as if we would be stalled at that encounter and could not proceed to do anything else if our minds did not fill in an explanation — any explanation, even an absurd one. And back in our more superstitious past, we ascribed those mysteries to magic or the world of the spirit.

I have no knowledge that there is a web that the little fellow is climbing up and down. You may offer a more learned explanation.

What a marvelous engineer he is. In the few minutes since I settled in, he has evidently spun the single strand of web between my board and the twig, and now he glides up to it to his perch, where he pauses, then moves away along the twig. I must be careful not to move the board too drastically and break the web. Perhaps he will descend again to visit me.

A very nice spring rain is coming down now, exactly what we want this time of year; especially in these drought conditions. These are the April showers, and they are arriving in May.

I notice that the birds don't mind the rain. A little marsh wren scoots across my path as I approach the water. Even though I have sought cover now, the red-wing still warbles away in the cattails, as if he rather exults in the rain.

A cardinal is still nearby but she is mostly quiet. She is busy primping and preening, fluffing her feathers for a bath in the rain. Ah, two mallards sail in and land on the marsh pond to complete my day.

The constant very faint rumble comes to this place from far away to the northwest. It suggests the sound that comes with heat lightning, as we have just come through a very hot summer day. The thermometer registered 84 degrees in the shade.

A red squirrel scoots across my boot and up a nearby Norway pine. He perches on the stump of a dead limb and chatters away, scolding me as if to say, "This is my place! What do you mean by invading my domain? Go away! Go away!"

I'm ensconced in my downy portable lawn chair, however, enjoying the woods immensely and figure he'll get over it soon and go back to gathering supplies for winter as he should be doing. But he is a sassy little fellow

Suddenly the pines are alive with chickadees, advancing through the upper limbs in front of me, like an aviary army. They're headed for my feeders. They don't fool me.

I've scattered some crackers a few yards in front of me, and mama chipmunk has come out boldly and sits up on her haunches sideways to me, nibbling on a cracker and keeping one eye on me to be sure that I'm no danger. Now her young ones, half her size, join her and share the feast.

One little fellow holds the cracker in his tiny paws and twirls it slowly and deftly as he nibbles away at its edges. He pays no attention to me, as if I'm just part of the terrain, and I'm slightly insulted that I don't loom as a more imposing figure in front of him. But life is new to him, and nothing as yet has the tag of "danger" attached to it. I wish that could always be.

Clouds. The wind comes up. A sudden squall off the lake. I am sent scurrying for cover, with chair and notebook under my arms, to the protection of the screen house.

The wind dies. The heavens open up, and rain pummels down upon the earth, like someone had let a great lake pour down upon us, all at once. The rain creates rivulets in the sandy soil, small streams all racing for lower ground, where it pools and is quickly drunk up by the thirsty ground, descending to the great aquifer under us and allowing us to shake ourselves off and begin again, dry but refreshed. The rain is like a little R&R from the busy world.

I trundle out again with equipment under my arm, and set up once more in a renewed world. A loon sings out his laughter on the lake to announce the end of the downpour, heckling us as if to say, "Who cares about getting wet? For some of us, getting wet is a part of everyday life!"

It reminds me that someone once said that humans may be descended from fish, by our shape. Perhaps next time I must just stand out in the rain and let it refresh me.

The forest seems to settle down, as if to cool off a bit. The greens begin to turn to grays.

Now suddenly a remarkable event takes place as the darkness settles into the woods. All of a sudden I hear the sound of countless thousands of insects — mosquitoes perhaps — all about me in every direction. What is remarkable is that a moment ago, although I was listening intently to evening sounds, I did not hear them at all. It is as if on cue, someone turned them on.

What is happening? Are they coming out or hatching out? What an all-pervasive sound!

The wail of the loons on Ham Lake behind me signals the coming on of night. I catch the late-evening view of the darkening lake through the pine trees. The rumble of the thunder is a little closer. It is time to call it a day.

*****

Red squirrel descends from a tall pine and eyes me. But he doesn't scold me this time and hustles back up the tree to his work.

The mallards exploded off the water into the air, detecting before we did the swooping approach of a bald eagle. A moment later we saw the eagle, who braked and then rose up over the pines and disappeared, as if neither we nor the ducks were to his taste.

The mallards affected no great alarm and after flapping about and honking a bit just a few feet up in the air, settled back down where they had been and continued to sun themselves and hunt for food. It was as if to say they were not to be buffaloed by that white-headed rascal and only wished to protest his intrusion. After all, this was their place for the afternoon, and they were not intimidated in the least.

My wife and I had paddled into this small lagoon on Leech Lake in our canoe. We came around a point and were surprised to discover ourselves breathtakingly close to the mallards. We quit paddling and just drifted. They seemed undisturbed by us. We just sat and watched them for quite some time.

Then the eagle struck. But they settled down near us again, as if we were not there. It seems strange. Sometimes wild creatures seem desperately frightened by us humans. Then at other times, they quietly accept us as if we were one of them. It is a great gift they give us when they do this. Those are golden moments in our experience of the forest.

Later, as I was sitting in my downy lawn chair in the woods, a blue jay landed some distance away in the Norway pines, heralding his presence with his call. A good breeze was coming off the lake on my back. The sun was about to set, peering through the trees on my left.

I whistled a poor imitation of the jay's call and called him in. Others fluttered about in the upper terraces of the pines, as if checking out the commotion. He came to a spot right above me on a pine. He cocked his head and eyed me for a few moments. He apparently decided I was a poor excuse for a blue jay, and he and his companions flew off.

I spread a few crackers in front of me on the ground. Then when I left for a few minutes to clean some fish, the little woodland rascals came and cleaned them all up, as if they'd left a sign behind them on the spot: "No show for you today, big friend. Ta-ta!"

Yesterday a huge crow landed on the ground some distance in front of me. They always look huge, somehow, when you see them up close. He stood sideways, eyeing me.

Then he sidled sideway toward me, much like a prankish cat on stiff legs does, when he's making a mocking attack in play.

"You want the crackers, not me. You don't fool me, old friend," I said to myself. At about six feet, however, he decided that I loomed too large as a threat, and he took flight. Too bad. I liked him.

Some ducks land on the lake near me now. The lakefront is quiet. It's dusk. They waddle up on the sand and hunker down for the night.

******

A torrential rain gave the forest a good soaking yesterday. It found me grabbing my lawn chair and books and heading for cover.

However there is something just cussed enough in me to make me don raincoat and rain pants and head out into the deluge with a pointed shovel, and ditch along the boathouse to carry water away. Remind me on a nice, sunny day that I could just as well be out doing that ditching and enjoying the sunshine.

(But where would be the sport in that? I have the same kind of cussed inclination to go out into snowstorms, or to walk through the midnight woods without a flashlight. It must have something to do with a desire to get in touch with what nature has to offer.)

The morning after is a wonder to behold. I totter out with notebook and chair under arm and coffee cup in hand, and head for my favorite spot at the base of some giant Norway pines and some less-giant white oaks. The woods are alive with a new freshness. In this sandy soil, no water stands about, of course, so the forest floor is very navigable.

A few drops of water still linger on the white oak leaves within reach of the chair. The sunshine breaking through the tree cover soon dries them.

The two aforementioned trees remind me of a program we took in at the nature center in Itasca State Park years ago that turned around my thinking on the growth of trees. We do the best we can as humans to observe nature, but our problem is that our lives are far too short to get perspective.

On Templar Point on Leech Lake I was observing (without realizing it then) a relatively-young area of tree growth, perhaps only 60 or 70 years old. I observed taller deciduous trees towering over the area and pines struggling up through the leaf-made shade to reach the sunlight. The conifers were healthy but small.

Over the 45 years we were there, I observed the conifers grow tall and strong and begin to reach the sunlight over the deciduous trees (elms, birch, poplar, basswood, maples, oak and the like). I concluded that the conifers (Norway and white pines and white cedar mostly) were destined to be the denizens of the crowning state of growth in the forest. During that time I was to discover how wrong I was.

At the Itasca Nature Center we learned from video illustrations how the crowning stage of growth was to be those maples and oaks that would one day dominate the pines.

If only nature could whisper these truths to me — truths that I could not live long enough to see.

But now let's take a break from all of this serious talk and have a little fun. We go down to the lakeshore.

Have you had a clam race yet? You haven't? Well, this is the season to have one.

Now how does one go about such a thing? Let me tell you; a few simple instructions are all you will need.

First you find a couple of clam tracks in the shallow water along a sandy lakeshore. In case looking for clam tracks isn't your frequent activity, a clam track is a single, shallow groove (he's only one-footed, you know), left in the soft sand that tells you a clam has passed this way. You follow that path (it may be only a few yards) until it comes to an end and disappears down into the sand.

The clam has buried himself in the sand to take a little rest. So gently, very gently, you dig down at that point (if you're lucky, he may be still slightly visible above the sand) with your fingers and gently scoop him out.

Then you take him up into very shallow water, a foot or two from shore, and gently insert him into the sand a little, foot down (naturally; who wants to start a race with his foot up?) and facing forward, out into the lake. Be sure the valve hinge is to the back. After that you find a second clam that will be his competitor, follow the same procedure, and place him next to the first.

Now a clam race is not something where you buy a bag of popcorn, sit down and wait for the action to begin. It won't even do any good to fire a starting pistol. Clams have no truck with such things.

You can come back a day later, mark their progress and declare a winner. No need to worry that they'll have disappeared over the horizon. You'll find them three or four yards out into the lake at most.

One of the downsides of clam races is that clams have a very poor sense of direction. They start off fine for a few feet, then one heads off south and the other heads off east.

Well, there you have it; a clam race. I know. You're going to say, "I strongly suspect that Jim is pulling our collective leg. Clam races, indeed!"

I know how you feel. I had a dear Ojibwe friend from Old Agency, Bill Butcher (Bill and his wife Doris have both passed away now) who used to share woods lore with me. It sounded so logical, but afterward I'd wonder, was Bill pulling my leg? Sometime, perhaps, I can regale you with stories that Bill told me. I'd be convinced they were fiction, and then later I'd hear or read something that sounded very similar to what Bill told me.

Someday I'll be gone, and you'll hear someone speak of clams, and you'll say, "You know, it sounds very much like what Jim told us!"

******

The city of Fargo has created a riparian area of native grasses and plants that are allowed to grow wild and free along the Red River, which I think is truly a delight. I am sitting on the edge of it at the moment, the demarcation line between mowed areas and the wild grasses.

The city accomplished this, but not without some controversy. Protesters argued that the area would be infested with mosquitoes. But it has proven not to be a problem.

The riparian area stretches 28 yards ahead of me to the river. A line of willows and small shrubs borders the stream, and tall grasses and flowers stretch back to where I sit, which includes the sea of wood asters.

Experts argue that this kind of unmowed native border is good for the health of the river. It cleanses the run-off water before it enters the river.

A band of goldfinches flit among the small trees that border the river. They play some distance from me, but their bright yellow and black markings are unmistakable. I can hear their sweet piping sounds in the asters near me, but they are playing hide-and-seek and remain out of sight.

A giant elm tree, four feet in diameter at its base, towers above and spreads its leafy boughs in a canopy over me. Its base stands only four yards from me. Nuthatches parade up and down its trunk, searching for insects.

The great branches of the elm spread out 12 yards in all directions from the base of the tree. They tell me that the root system of such a tree spreads out as far underground as the branch system above. That means those roots spread halfway from where I sit to the river and provide tremendous aid in holding the soil alongside the river. What a marvelous system these huge trees are, providing shelter, sustenance, homes for animal life, beauty for the landscape and protection for the soil.

Ah! A red squirrel in the tree has discovered me and is scolding me. It is time for me to leave for the day.

A female wood duck sails into an ash tree across the river from me, a tree with its feet still in the waters of the receding flood. I grab my binoculars and try to spot her among the branches, but with no luck.

Then I spot the cause of her approach and the low kind of whistle call she makes: Mr. Wood Duck paddles sportily on the tide nearby, showing off his flashy red, black and white colors. Soon she apparently can't resist him any longer, and she glides down out of the tree and lands on the water a few feet from him. Then she paddles right on by for 15 or 20 feet, as if he wasn't what she had in mind at all.

He takes the bait, turns around and heads for her. But he paddles right on by, as if she wasn't what he had in mind at all. Two can play this game.

She joins him, and they let the Red River drift them downstream 30 feet or so. She takes a notion to stroll up onto the grassy bank that rolls gently down into the river.

He joins her and mischievously whacks her on the side with his beak, like the grade school boy who can't think of a better way to encounter the cute little blond girl on the playground, than to whack her. Miss Wood Duck, however, takes umbrage at this (though only slightly, of course) and scoots into the water.

After a time, I spy them huddled together in a thicket on shore, a few inches from the water. I think it is the better part of discretion to turn my glasses away from them for a while and give them a little privacy.

The moon has just risen over the ash trees on the far bank — a full moon, a lover's moon. It stands rather strangely in the daytime sky, for the sun has not set yet. But it is beautiful, nevertheless.

The oaks nearby are slower to respond to spring. They are only flowering now and will need a few more days to start their leaves.

****

Eight turkey vultures stroll the mud flats just above the riverbank across the river from me. Another one sails gracefully among the nearby trees, back and forth, scouting out the situation before landing among the others.

A rooster sports about by one of the hens. She shows some interest, and then coyly prances around the bole of a big elm tree away from him.

The others sail high above the tall trees, catching the wings of the morning wind and barely seeming to need to move their wings as they sail back and forth in the updrafts, like creatures detached from the earth, hanging by a suspension all their own.

The river has politely receded to a level within its banks now, though it still looks a bit swollen. The flats just above the banks still look soggy and glisten with moisture in the morning sun. A pair of tiny kinglets plays among the willows on the river bank on my side of the river. They have me too much at a disadvantage, with the sun behind them, to tell whether they are golden or ruby crowned. One sits up saucily on a low branch and fluffs his feathers in the morning sun. The other darts about and the first one gives chase with a flashing of busy wings. Then they settle down again and perch awhile.

A cooper's hawk suddenly takes flight from a big spreading elm tree near me and heads for the river. I hadn't spotted him earlier when he arrived, unless he was here before I came and had roosted there for the night.

He swoops low over the kinglets, but they ignore him as he heads across the river. Likewise, a gaggle of mallards swimming near the far bank ignore him as he passes overhead and lights in a big ash tree near the shore.

He fluffs up his feathers, sporting his banded tail, as if seeking to summon up an improved, menacing image. At last he flies south along the river, perhaps seeking more timid prey.

I am surrounded by white oaks and American elms, which become more evident as their foliage advances. A band of low willows grace the river bank, with a few small scattered ash among them. A 70-foot lone spruce towers above the oaks nearby, perhaps a remnant of the days when humans lived on this side of the dike before the river pushed them back.

The turkey vultures have departed. I didn't see them take flight, so perhaps they have settled into the thicket near them to relax into the day.

*****

The wood anemone surrounds me at this spot in the woods by Ham Lake, where I find myself this morning. The sun is just breaking through the clouds, and it looks as if it might dispel those clouds.

A wonderful change that I hope to see in the anemone as it greets the morning sun is the opening of its petals into the exquisite little cinquefoil blossom. At the moment it is still closed from the cool night air into the white nubbin that is its night form. Its change hasn't happened, so I shall have to be patient. Stay tuned.

This is a wonderful time for woodland flowers. I went down by a wet area nearby to see if I might see some marsh marigolds, but no luck in that spot.

Yesterday we saw them in a marsh alongside the road west of here — a sea of them, gorgeous to behold. We picked a small bouquet to grace our table with their deep gold blossoms, mostly five petals but sometimes six.

Some lilacs festooned the roadside, too; we wondered if they might have been remnants of a former farmstead, now long gone. Many of the lilacs were in that not-quite-open stage when they are most fragrant.

But the most delightful was a curious and plentiful little blossom that is out now called the pussy toes. It never opens into a very showy blossom, but from the top it looks exactly like its name.

Along the roadside now one also sees the hoary puccoon in their gay clusters by their shiny leaves. Their brilliant gold petals fairly glisten in the afternoon sun.

The woodland birds serenade me this morning. They answer when I call to them, but mostly they refuse to make appearances, and I am not good enough at the calls to identify them that way. A robin sings near me which, of course, any of us would identify. A catbird, with its varied calls, perches atop some low bush at a short distance. A chickadee chirps as he busies himself among some Norway pine boughs nearby. A common tern soars overhead, just up from the lake, and calls. But otherwise the songsters remain hidden.

How greened-out the forest has become from when I sat here a month ago. Then one could see a long way into the woods through the almost-bare branches and limbs. Now the woods have quite closed in around me with greenery.

Early this week we committed the ashes of a dear friend to a large lake south of here. They floated on the surface of the still lake that quiet sunny afternoon. Then they slowly began to disperse in an ever-widening pattern. I was reminded of how I am a part of all of this, and I return to it.

As soon as I had settled myself in the deep woods near Ham Lake, a phoebe greeted me with his two-note call (low-high, low-high), from the top of a tall Norway pine. I was able to put my binoculars on him and spot his black beak and forked tail. He is gone at the moment, and whether he will come back to serenade me more, we will see.

His notes are a little higher than the easiest range for me, beginning at a C. He begins a little higher, perhaps at an E, with a five-note interval; perhaps at E-B, E-B. I shall have to check that, as I am not that good at identifying notes. But it is a lovely call.

Promptly a crow sails as silently as a ghost through the pines, 50 yards in front of me, defying observation, had I not had my eyes on that spot at the moment. I can't help remarking on the graceful beauty of his flight, regardless of the fact that he is too common to be a favorite.

A moment later, he swings back through, as if toying with me, always silent, unlike his usual raucous nature. A third time he returns, and this time he lands in the pine and cocks his head at me. But before I can get my glasses on him, he frisks away like a big tease. Now I hear his call. I can see why he doesn't make it among the top 10 bird singers ...

Another songster whistles at me with his five-note call, all on one note, perhaps about a B. He has sung to me for the last few days and answers my call when I whistle back; but he refuses to let himself be seen.

A volume that has been helpful to me is one my daughter Julie gave me. Judy Pelikan's "The Music of Wild Birds" is a volume that I warmly recommend. It covers 50 birds commonly seen by birdwatchers, a number that any of us can get our minds around. I looked at the 50, and the only one with this five-note call was the wrens, most accurately the winter wren, but also possibly our familiar house wren.

The spot where I sit has enough sunlight shining through the pines and white oaks onto the forest floor that the poison ivy has prospered. It often is not plentiful in the deep woods.

I know this plant is hardly a welcome visitor for humans. However, I am rather a friend of poison ivy. Perhaps I wouldn't be if I were more affected by it.

Speaking of friends, my phoebe friend has declined to return. I shall have to wait for him for another day.

*****

The song sparrow, with the bold black spot on his vest, seems bent upon entertaining me with his song and antics as I sit under the big elm in the unmowed riparian area that stretches 80 feet up from the bank of the Red River.

At the moment he is singing his heart out from the top of a low clump of ash trees on the river bank, with his one high note and five lower notes.

He sits jauntily up at the top of a small, leafy branch that sways in the breeze, opens his beak upward and sings out lustily as if he were serenading the beautiful, mild sunny day. He seems in no hurry to move on.

Earlier he sat on some old, stiff brown stalks of last year's grasses that still poke up among the fresh, green new growth. He sang to me there near eye level and about 70 feet away.

I tried to call him in, and he approached to within about 30 feet, cocking his head, eyeing me and singing as he came. At that point he must have decided that I made a rather miserable-looking song sparrow, and he headed back toward the river bank.

Then I discovered the real reason for his departure. He joined a lady friend among some low brush.

The woods are fully leafed out now, though a little late in arriving, and summer is fully upon us. The first flowering has appeared; great patches of yellow among the green of the wheat grass. I am thinking it is hedge mustard, but I will have to check on that. It has exquisite little bell-shaped blossoms, no more than two millimeters across and gathered in clusters of about 15 blossoms.

Ash and willow line the river bank, but only in patches, so one can still clearly see the easy-flowing river. Most of them are bent north, having been pushed by the ice floes on the flooded river.

A giant willow to my left reaches up 42 feet into the air, with a four-foot thick trunk at its base and in a cluster of four such trunks. It stands unbowed by the battering of ice floes or even a giant windstorm that smashed many trees in our area a few weeks ago.

Suddenly I am being treated to a Brewer's blackbird. Or is it? It is perched on a bare branch 30 feet from me and has held there long enough for me to get a good look at its all-black body and brown head. It is preening itself and enjoying the sun. I must check on that ... nope. No such luck. It is the lowly cowbird.

Song sparrow still sings nearby. Perhaps his lady friend has not chosen him, and he must sing for another. I wish him well. His lovely song deserves such wishes.

The river has overflowed its banks again. I emptied three inches of water out of my rain gauge this morning.

The current flows much more swiftly out in the center now than it did a few days ago; more slant to it now as it flows north. We'll see if there is a change in the level of it by the hour as we watch

Birds play about and sing in the forest everywhere, which is fun to see. Within minutes, I spot goldfinches, wood peewees, downy woodpeckers, red-winged blackbirds and even a perky song sparrow that sings to me from the top of a tall weed 20 feet away.

The mowed areas are populated with our most common bird friends: robins, starlings, grackles, cowbirds, feasting on whatever such areas have to offer after a good rain. They hardly seem to be bothered by me watching them as I walk by. I notice an interesting absence of waterfowl on all of this water. They've obviously moved north to their breeding areas.

Sitting in an area where I sat last winter gives me a good opportunity to confirm the identity of the trees, now that they have leaves on them, where I only had bare woods in midwinter. I must try to match the leaves with their bark so that hopefully I am a bit more ready when winter comes.

I was surprised at the risen river, as we thought, hopefully, that the flooding was over for the season. The spot where I sat last week by the big elm was 80 feet from the river. Today I could still have set up my chair at the base of the tree, but my feet would have been in water.

Yesterday I spoke with a friend in Cookstown, Ireland, and told her about our unusually wet season. She said they have had over two months of unseasonably wet weather. I am wondering if these abnormalities are global.

The edge of the river has receded six inches on a shallow slope in the last hour. Perhaps there is hope for summer to come yet.

******

A cottonwood seed drifts by not 20 feet in front of me, five feet in the air, headed north on a soft south breeze.

It drifts on for another 40 yards before it settles down among the 30-inch high wheat grass, headed down for the moist soil here along the Red River. Half a dozen such seeds have floated by me in the last half hour. They've apparently come from quite a distance, for the most I can see is perhaps one or two cottonwoods a quarter mile north.

They will, of course, not sprout and prosper. They will simply give their mortal remains to the ecology, for this unmown riparian area that stretches up 80 yards from the river bank is dominated by the tall grasses.

What causes one set of flora to dominate a region? Even the mighty white oak must give way to the lowly wheat grass in certain places.

Where I sit, the wheat grass stands tall on either side of me. Except for the giant elm at my back, I see only a massive willow 50 yards north and a big green ash 100 yards south. The grasses flourish and dominate the area between. They let you know that this is prairie country, and they are in charge.

These large trees remind me that long ago, within my memory, this strip to the river was mowed. Tree seedlings were mowed down regularly, and large trees were allowed to grow.

When one drives out across the prairie country, one occasionally sees shelter belts standing alone without buildings. They are the remnants of old farmsteads, where the buildings are gone. The trees are the energetic efforts of settlers, perhaps Norwegians, who sought to surround themselves with reminders of the trees of their homeland.

Indeed, to anyone visiting one of these farmsteads in the days when they were occupied, they were a warm haven out of the chill winds on the open prairies. I recall one that was completely surrounded by a thick shelter belt. It felt like a different climate inside that haven.

Although I am not Norwegian, as many Minnesotans and North Dakotans are — I am of British extraction — all of this made me realize how much we northern Europeans are at home in the woodlands. There is something friendly to us about a tree. European settlers in the United States loved to plant trees around their farmsteads and water and nurture them.

I feel that we humans are important to the ecology of the planet in positive ways, but we have important lessons to learn from those species that have been here before us.

I recall someone telling me once that, allowed to stand by themselves without humans to tend them, these grasses would ultimately dominate these shelter belt trees and take over the areas on which these trees once stood. Old cottonwoods would ultimately drop millions of floating seeds fruitlessly and simply offer their remains to the ecology of the grassland.

Two more seeds have drifted by me, ready to offer themselves to this grassland.

One small green worm is my only visitor in the woods at the moment on so hot and muggy a July day that the sultriness seems to hang around one like a pall. This little visitor trooping up and down my arm can't be more than a half inch long, moving like what we used to call inchworms when we were kids, contracting and extending himself with each advance, as if he were measuring out an inch with each step (or, in this case, a half inch).

At Home in the Woodlands

Worms in the woods — that is, the kind that crawl around above ground on leaves and branches — never cease to amaze me. Of the hundreds and hundreds I've seen, they never seem to be the same. It's as if when God started making worms, He decided, just for sport, not to repeat Himself in order to give entomologists a real run for their money. And, by the same token, it gave endless delight to those of us who love the woods.

This little fellow, for example, boasts a nice, translucent green all down his short length, except for a dark spot partway along, as if he'd just had his dinner and it hadn't quite passed through. He looks like one long alimentary canal, but he does have some sort of perception at the head, for he stops every once in a while and reaches his head up to check if anything's above him.

A butterfly just landed on my lapboard. He had fluttered about my head for a bit and then landed on a napkin that I had been using to mop my brow in this sultry weather. Perhaps he detected a scent in the napkin that attracted him.

Now he has alighted on the paper that I'm writing on and is taking a break on the word "landed" just ahead of this. He's such a nervous fellow that I gladly grant him a rest from his flitting.

He doesn't sport any fancy color like a monarch. But he is an attractive brown with black markings in it.

When he lands on the pine three feet to my left, he is almost invisible against that reddish-brown bark. He's obviously not into attracting predators by sporting fancy colors.

It occurs to me by his visit that he is reminding me, "I was once a small worm like the one you are entertaining." (Could he have been a larva very like this green fellow?) Perhaps that is why you don't see us woodland worms more often than you do."

My little green friend has crawled off my arm and disappeared, perhaps onto some white oak leaves brushing my lapboard. Only the brown butterfly flits about like a ghost to remind me of my friend.

I am struck by how woods change and yet seem to stay the same. In the few hours that I am sitting here in the warm sun on a pleasant day with recent rain, I could rise up at the end of it and conclude that nothing had changed. Yet almost everything about me is living, and so everything would have changed, albeit to the slightest degree.

As I come here from week to week, I would be able to see change, if I were careful to notice it. But I would have to trace it in the smallest plant or part of a plant to be able to detect it. In the early spring, of course, the changes are huge, so they would be much easier to trace

To set myself to this task, I have selected a small plant, a wild raspberry, next to my chair. I have put a white cord loosely around its base to discover it easily again when I return. For I have found that small plants and their neighbors have a way of working mischief on their observers by apparently transforming themselves into something else and leaving the poor observer baffled by their disappearance. So the cord is sort of like a lasso to keep the critter in the corral.

I did this sort of thing with a death camass plant 20 years ago in the Yukon. I was able to trace it from its first appearance in spring.

This little raspberry shoot is now 10 inches tall, with 18 leaves showing. The largest are probably almost full-grown, measuring perhaps an inch across and two inches long. They appear in unfailing triplets, which makes for easy counting.

The tiny triplet at the top is an exact replica of the full-grown leaves, with the exquisite exactness and freshness of a baby's little hand and fingers, compared to an adult's. The question arises in my mind, how warm and life-giving would the weather need to be for me to see change within hours? Sigh! I am like the impatient film-watcher who wants to see plants grow by progressions of still shots.

The critters are more cooperative. I had placed a handful of niblets at the base of the pine five feet to the right of me, and they had completely cleaned them up during the week; not a crumb left. I've placed another handful for them today. Of course, they aren't rewarding me with a view of them when they come to snatch the goodies.

*****

A week later, back at Ham Lake, I walk from the lake toward the woods. Ah! Three hawks float on the updrafts in the openings in the pines straight above me. They are falcon-winged, as opposed to the broad wings of the buteos. They have black wing bands. I must identify them later. No — they are not hawks, but ospreys!

As soon as I settle into the woods, a green-throated blue warbler female treats me to a visit 15 feet in front of me at eye level in the thick deciduous undergrowth.

She perches on a light branch at the saucy angle of warblers and eyes me for a moment. Then she moves off before I have a chance to get the glasses on her to identify the telltale white wing spot.

What a winsome event. I wouldn't have seen her had I not glanced at that bush at that exact moment. She moves through as silently as a ghost. I can't get her to respond to the "zur" note of her call. Will she treat me to another visit before I leave?

I hear the trill of another warbler to the right, lovely and dropping in pitch. It could be the myrtle warbler, but he won't present himself to my view.

I spoke of change the last time I sat here a week ago. The little wild raspberry plant I had marked with a white loop now stretches up 12 inches instead of 10 and sports 21 leaves, having added a trio of leaflets. And as I suspected, it tried to escape my notice. A broad plantain leaf has stretched itself over the white loop, concealing it to the casual view. One leaf trio is broken and hanging limp. From what? Another plant, an animal passing by, some wind?

This place is just the same, enough so that I can find this spot again and put down my chair where it was and recognize my surroundings. And yet it is all changed, every bit of it, and did I not take special notice, I would invariably miss that change. In fact, it is likely not changing just week by week, but moment by moment, were I astute enough to notice it. The one eternal fact is that change that passes through us like a wand and causes us to be; and then to be no more.

And one day I shall be here no longer, and perhaps loggers will have come and harvested these stately Norways (God forbid!) and left scrub.

The other day I was looking at these pines. I asked my wife, should we be harvesting these pines (some of them tower up to 180 feet in the air), rather than just let them grow old and die and fall down?

To which question she answered, NO. It was an unequivocal NO, which a wife will deliver from time to time, offering no chance for debate.

So they will grow old and die and offer homes for birds and animals for a few years and then fall down and, perhaps, we will cut them up and use their pieces. And other pines already coming up will take their place. C'ste la vie.

I hear now the eight-note whistle of a wren. But I see him only briefly.

The warbler will not treat me to another visit. So I must sigh and hope for it another day.

*****

A beautiful monarch butterfly flits by me where I sit. Now I see him sailing a bit on a stiff breeze from the east, the direction that I'm facing. Now he's alighted in some little bluegrass ahead of me. I say "little," but it stands two or three feet high. He's disappeared for the moment; perhaps having some lunch or taking a siesta on this hot, muggy afternoon. I wouldn't blame him.

I've heard that these monarchs migrate in the autumn 2,500 miles, from here down into Mexico, to a place where they congregate by the thousands, perhaps millions, as if gathering in a great monarch convention in warmer climes. There is a mystery about them.

The other day my wife and our grandsons brought in a chrysalis they had found near the lakeshore. It had attached itself to the back of the webbing of one of our lawn chairs sitting there.

They wanted to watch it metamorphose, but the boys were afraid a kingfisher or nuthatch or something else would come along and gobble it up. So they asked Grandma if they could cut off a piece of the webbing to which it was attached and take it indoors.

Grandma agreed to sacrifice her chair, as long as they didn't sever the whole webbing strap. In they bore their prize and placed it on a stick that was placed upright in a glass jar with a lid with holes in it.

I thought it would be a long process, but it wasn't more than a few days before a beautiful monarch butterfly emerged from the chrysalis, truly a metaphor for the resurrection. I say beautiful, but in truth at first it looked like a wetted-down newborn baby and not so gorgeous.

However it quickly clung to the stick, rested there and took its own sweet time drying off and gradually transforming itself into the beautiful creature it was meant to become.

Quite a change. It's a good reminder that as gorgeous as you and I are today, we, too, once were the mucky little beings that only a mother could love.

We kept the little fellow for a number of hours until he seemed fully developed into his monarchical self. Then we removed the lid and took him, jar and all, to a sheltered spot out of the wind and hot sun and set the jar down.

We had hoped to watch him crawl out of the jar, stretch himself and take wing, but when we returned a short time later, he was gone. We wished him well upon his way.

Although we didn't see his first flight, perhaps it was just as well. We had peeked in on enough of the intimacy of his beginnings for one day.

*****

Back on the banks of the Red River again — or at least as near as one can get to the banks at this time. What a strange water world greets me for this time of the year.

I am sitting 20 yards up from the water's edge at the moment, and that edge is perhaps 30 yards up from the usual river bank. The water from shore to shore now stretches more than 75 yards, at least half again the usual river width.

The talk I hear everywhere is that the city fathers are greatly concerned about what this will mean for flooding in the spring. I'm not exactly clear how the two are connected, for after all the river will likely go down by — oops! That's right, it's already August.

A family of seven blue-winged teal greeted me as I came here, about 50 yards to the left of where I am sitting. The river's edge actually scoops in further there than where I am. The teal head for the water (they'd been resting ashore) when I arrived, but they've all returned to land again, figuring that I don't seem to be too great a threat.

They've returned to land in a rather bewildered fashion, as if to suggest they hadn't really been intimidated at all. Two of them bathe themselves, spreading their wings and feathers, and getting wet all over with a lot of splashing. One ducks his head and puts his tail into the air like a puddle duck.

The 50-foot stately old elm that I actually sit under at this time of the year has her feet in the water now. I worry about how much these fine old trees can take this feet-in-water business, but some of them look to have been around for a half-century or more, and perhaps have experienced these elongated floods before.

A half-century did I say? I've been here nearly that long, and I don't remember them being much smaller than this when I came. The age of these great giants must be impressive. Of course, how good is our human-tree memory? Unless we carve our initials into them, are we looking at the same trees, when we return years later?

A half-dozen big crows are putting up quite a ruckus in the big trees to the right of me. It seems likely that a large predator, a hawk or owl, has flown in without my noticing it, and the corvidae have made it their business to harass him out of the neighborhood. I can't spot the culprit at the moment, but by the sound of things, it seems they've moved him up river a ways. A great blue heron sails in and lands.

Two of the crows flew down among the teal, as if to check out if the latter had found any food of interest. The teal waddle among them, obviously accepting their company.

The river flows swiftly, yet seems to remain unchanged. One wonders from where all of this water is coming.

*****

Today finds me a half a globe away from home, in the woods of Scotland. Why not? It is a lesson learned that one can be at home in the woodlands anywhere on the planet. Of course, I must admit that one would need special skills which I do not possess to be at home in the land of the tigers.

And now a small predator is treating me to a performance not 80 feet out from me at about 45 degrees. As I looked I could have sworn he was tethered to an invisible wire and otherwise hanging motionless for a count of 15, giving me a good chance to observe him before he folded his wings and dove into the deep grass after something.

A class act! Worthy to qualify for the Edinburgh Drama Festival which, as a matter of fact, has brought me to this fair city.

My companions were good enough to release me from theater going for a few hours and sent me off into this mountain near Edinburgh called Arthur's Seat.

I was able to get a good look at the small predator in that time with the sun behind me lighting him beautifully as he hovered, framed against the red grays of the cliffs of Arthur's Seat behind him. He reminded me, with his orange colorings, of our sparrow hawk or redtail. (Do I recall someone from royal history or literature — could it have been Scottish history — referred to as the sparrow hawk?)

Now I suddenly hear a low hooting as an owl high on the cliff in front of me. I can spot where he is by the sound, but he refuses to present himself to my view. His call is a trio of notes in a low fourth, perhaps C-F-C. It would be haunting at night. No, it is a quintet: C-F-C (rest) C-C.

A showy magpie has sailed in and landed on a rock outcropping 60 yards in front of me. Now he has sailed in closer into a small weather-beaten tree that I am at a loss to identify. Now a crow has joined him, as if to check whether he might have discovered a bit of carrion he might like to share.

The redtail hovers near me again, not 30 feet to my left. What an amazing bird. He seems to catch the strong drafts of wind I felt as I came over the top of this pass, and uses them to hover as long as he wishes.

Is he perhaps the predator to whom the crow objected earlier? Perhaps he flew a little too close to their nesting area. However, they are quiet now.

Ah! A predator hawk has invaded the cliff realms of the crow, and the crows are busy bedeviling him relentlessly out of the area with their customary squawking and general ruckus. Life is the same the world over.

One might guess I was sitting on shores of Leech Lake watching this drama, except of course, that Leech Lake has nothing except the high banks on Templar Point to call cliff realms. Instead, now you find me among the gorse in bonnie Scotland near Edinburgh — at home in the woodlands.

*****

Today I'm looking at the countryside in the far north of England, south of Carlisle. Summertime in England! What woods there are grace the hills above the pastureland where blackfaced sheep graze contentedly.

Doves coo on the edge of woodlands near the habitations of humans. Their cooing is a low trio of notes.

A flock of dark-colored birds, perhaps two dozen of them, wheels across the edge of the pastureland and settles into the trees. Folks identify them simply as blackbirds, so perhaps that is enough for us to name them.

The woods seem to be mostly hardwoods like oak, but I would need to study them more to know. Willows prosper along the water courses.

Great white gulls soar and glide back and forth across the land, particularly near human habitations. They appear very much like our herring gulls but with more black coloration near the forepart of their bodies. And the ever-present crows (are they world-wide?) perch upon fence lines as if waiting for something to happen that would attract them.

It's always a challenge to identify birds overseas, because not everyone takes an interest in them. I recall one time on the streets of London observing many small birds hopping about in the gutters that I immediately identified as English sparrows. I thought, "This is a chance to find out if the

English call this bird 'English'." Perhaps it is only a name we [in America] have attached to them.

So I buttonholed a passerby on the crowded sidewalk, a little lady about five feet tall, and asked her for the name of the bird I pointed to. Her accent was somewhat unintelligible to me, and she seemed puzzled why anyone would ask about such a ridiculous little creature. At last, after some effort, I was finally able to wrestle out of her words, "That's a dit." "A dit?" I asked. "Yea, a dit," she replied with authority.

It occurs to me now that she was probably saying, "Tit," like the English bird called the blue tit. And she simply threw all small birds into that category. So at that moment I was unable to expand my English bird knowledge. I would have to be satisfied with the name "dit" for the time being.

It also occurred to me that every person is an ornithologist in his own right. I see a bird repeatedly, and even if I know nothing about birds, I give it a name, so that I can refer to it when talking to someone.

Moreover, in a way, I am being a scientist, for I am observing characteristics that are similar from one bird to another, and I am developing a category and giving it a name. All that our most eminent ornithologists have done beyond that is to make more observations and to develop more categories. Let's hear it for the "Dit" lady.

The dove has ceased his fluttering about and has come to roost for the night. His cooing continues but only occasionally. He is settling in for a good night's sleep.

*****

At Home in the Woodlands

I'm back home once again, enjoying the woods and neighborhood. A phoebe, with its indistinct wing bars, flits about in a slender green ash tree 50 feet in front of me on the banks of the Red River. He moves about from one branch to another, seemingly dissatisfied with first one perch, then another. I look for some kind of particular business he might be about, such as a search for insects, but he seems to be about no business at all and is just enjoying the late summer sun. Perhaps he will reward me with a view of some more purposeful activity later.

The river has receded back below its banks again, like a good river. I guess I shouldn't gainsay its right to flood. After all, this whole basin belongs to it, and we humans have only encroached and pretended it is ours.

A big splash on the far side of the river attracts my attention. I used to see beaver activity, and the sound brought that to mind. I've wondered why I haven't seen them for several years. Most likely I would need to come down here in the evening, which was when I saw them. Also I remember sitting on the shores of Templar Point on Leech Lake and seeing them swim by in the evenings.

A few weeks ago I remarked on some excellent viewing of the sparrow hawk in Edinburgh, Scotland, and I referred to it as the redtail. I need to correct that. I should have said kestrel. My apologies to raptor lovers.

Our American variety does, indeed, have a rufous red tail, but the tail of the European kestrel isn't even red; it is blue-gray. Moreover, a red tail to us would refer to the buteos known as the red-tailed hawk. The kestrel is not broad-winged, but falcon-like.

Our great bird mentor, Roger Tory Peterson, opts for a return to the European terms for hawks — harrier, peregrine, merlin and kestrel. He feels we've given beneficial hawks a bad rap by lumping all hawks together.

The trees that grace the riverbank directly ahead of me, where I saw the phoebe, are something to behold. "Grace" is hardly the appropriate word, for they are more like the ugly growths that imprisoned Beowolf's Grendl, before he was released to go marauding about the countryside.

These trees, two spindly green ash clumps and one tall willow clump, are bent and twisted, leaning downriver by the annual attack of spring ice over the years. The upriver clump is totally dead but still stands and has become the climbing poles for Virginia creepers. The other two struggle on, battered but alive and still holding the river bank.

And the phoebe says they are just fine for him, as he sports about among their branches.

****

A great blue heron graces the far bank of the river about 80 yards in front of me, as I stand in the dew-damp morning grass scanning the far shore with my glasses. He greets me as a surprise as I catch him in my sweep, for he is so silent and so motionless that he does not betray himself. But he does not see me yet, so he moves now to preen himself a bit.

Now he discoveries me, and he eyes me with a stony glare. I move back slowly to the refuge of my chair, drop out of his view, and he relaxes. A few moments later he lifts himself into the air on his slow wing beats, and flies north along the course of the river not three feet above the surface of the water. He disappears.

A female common yellowthroat glides into the branches of the giant American elm that spreads its limbs above me, greeting me with her tcheep, tcheep, that almost sounds like a bleep, bleep to me this morning.

She confuses me for identification with her bland appearance, until her male partner joins her with his distinct domino mask and his witchety, witchety singing. He continues serenading me in full view of me, insisting upon my full attention.

The slow-moving Red River seems almost still this morning and had reflected the heron perfectly a few moments ago as he stood ankle-deep in the water. Only a passing dead leaf floating on the water surface belies that stiffness.

Two turkey vultures sail serenely overhead and light in a great dead tree on the far bank, joining two vultures that had already taken up residence there, without my having noticed them. Now two more join the group — a regular convention. What silent brooding creatures they are, how unlike my yellowthroat, who insists that I notice him. What brings the vultures here?

Several crows pass overhead above the vultures, and hardly seem to notice them. They obviously are not threatened by them as they are by predators — they are just a couple of fellow scavengers who could gladly join us over a little road kill. Now two vultures go and another returns. I could almost start singing the "Three Chartreuse Buzzards" song.

Now, I can't let that reference pass without rendering these lyrics for you:

Three chartreuse buzzards,
Three chartreuse buzzards,
Three chartreuse buh..h..zzards sitting in a dead tree;
Oh, look! One of them has flown a-way.
What a-shame.

Two chartreuse buzzards...

.... and so forth, until they begin to return, and are all back.

Just think; you might have gone to your grave never knowing of that song had you not read this passage. A friend made it into the high school glee club auditioning with that bird song.

The sun greeted me earlier, but now the clouds have overcast the sky. What are those clouds?

I would like to better understand the overcast clouds. I understand that the storm sequence of clouds for an approaching storm runs from cirrus to cirro-stratus to alto-stratus to stratus to nimbo-stratus, and at that point we begin to have a storm or some rain, which I am starting to experience now, and which may move me under cover.

However, what are those overcast clouds, really? In their early form they still had an identifiable fleecy or wavy form. But now they are simply a gray mantle.

A light rain begins. Old "domino mask" is undaunted by the rain, and keeps singing. But I am driven to cover, and shall have to abandon the field to him.

*****

Returning to the riverside two weeks later, I am amazed at the change in the plant life. Whereas the last time I was here I saw only the smallest beginnings of grasses, now the brome grass stands 46 inches tall and practically conceals me where I sit. All the trees are fully leafed out. It is as if someone has waved a magic green wand over the land. Now five deer appear.

The woods are alive with the sounds of songbirds as well. However they do not show themselves to me yet, and I am not adept enough at identifying them by songs to tell what they are. Among them, I hear the familiar trilling of the robin and the kak-kak of the grackle, but beyond that, I am stumped. It's quite maddening not to see them.

Ah! The crows have discovered a predator to my left and are setting up quite a ruckus. I had hoped they might drive him this way so I could see him, but it appears he is planning to sit tight with whatever dignity he can maintain. The crows seem to consider themselves the self-appointed guardians of the woods.

I was listening to see if I could detect the songs of either of these birds among those who sing nearby but won't reveal themselves. One of them sounds like the "zi-zi-zi" of the blackpoll warbler, the song rising and then diminishing in emphasis.

However, I do not hear among these sounds the "chu-wee" of the yellow-bellied flycatcher. Perhaps he has already migrated north.

The young green ash tree that I have been observing for several years to see if it would survive floods seems to have prospered. It is fully leafed out and now stands nine feet tall. It also enjoys several small cousin ash trees around it now.

The river has been gentle with the land (and with the student sandbaggers) in the last few years. We did have a brief flood a month ago, but that happened not because the river has been high, but because of a downpour of rain that lasted for three days when the land was still too frozen to absorb the water — and it ran off into the river, which then flooded. But it went down quickly and hardly disturbed the riparian area.

Big fleecy cumulus clouds mostly cover the sky, with the deep summer blue of the sky showing through in places. It is one of those idyllic summer days, pleasantly warm, and not too hot; an ideal northern day.

A yellow warbler swoops in and lands in the old dead ash tree 40 feet in front of me on the river bank, to start my afternoon. He darts into the big willow to my left and soon a dozen warblers join him and sport about among the branches.

I had been hearing them before I spotted them, for the yellow warblers were sounding off with their tsee-tsee-tsee. I find it difficult to whistle their notes and easier just to sound it through the teeth. Birders note their sound as "Sweet, sweet, I'm so sweet."

A nuthatch lands in the ash now and marches up and down the trunk. I suspect he finds the old trunk a good place for bugs and worms.

At Home in the Woodlands

These eight old dead ash trees continue to amaze me. They continue to stand on the river bank, year after year.

When I say old, I do not mean in age, for they all died young. They range from six to eight inches in diameter near their base.

They all lean to the north, the direction of the river flow, having been battered by the north-flowing ice, year after year in flood season. They stand 42 feet tall, bent but not broken.

A white-crowned sparrow lands in one of the trees. He has the eye line and the white crown, but they are less distinct than usual. He gives me a good long time to observe him.

The wheat grass stands four feet tall where I sit. It has prospered in the last week or two, with some heavy rains at first and then some good warm sunshine. And it was treated to a gentle flood this year, with ice departing quickly and the river gently rising, then quietly subsiding, leaving a thin layer of good old Red River Valley silt.

Some warm sunny days quickly dried the riparian area, and the stage was set for this healthy growth of wheat grass.

My small ash sapling, which I have observed for several seasons and which stands to my left, is also doing well. It stands over six feet tall. But is it strong enough to survive spring floods?

Now there's a sight. A young Cooper's hawk, with his yellowish-brown markings, flies across my field of vision and lands on a dead branch of a white ash across the river. He perches long enough for me to get a good look. Then he flies off, but awkwardly, like a youngster doing some of his first hunting.

And now a yellow-throat perches in an ash clump to my left. He gives me a chance to get a good look at his domino or black mask, and his bright yellow markings.

The evening settles in, but not without a lark sparrow appearing. His song gives me a bright send off for my day.

****

The summer moves along, and the warm days bring a mix of blue skies and dramatic clouds.

What a gorgeous big white fleecy cumulus cloud displays itself against the deep blue sky to the right, catching my eye. It seems it has bent so low to the earth that I could reach out, touch it and toss the fleece with my fingers.

I recall such displays from my childhood days, when youngsters out of school would lie on their backs and watch the cotton-white fleecy clouds sail by on a sea of blue sky and try to imagine what shapes they see. To me, if I might be such a boy again for a moment, this cloud is a great white bird with a crest like a jay. I'm sure young girls would also love such flights of imagination, but I have only the experience of my sort.

Now the cumulus clouds darken on their undersides and morph into nimbus clouds. The nimbus always mean storms or rain of some kind.

Sure enough, in a few moments, rain; and I am driven under cover. But only briefly, and now I am out again, drinking in quaffs of this delicious moisture-laden summer air.

The westerlies are bringing more such clouds, interspersed by these gorgeous, rich, deep blue patches of summer sky. So I shall likely be driven under cover again; so be it. But I see a summer turkey out yet.

Persistent soft summer rains have given us a rich greening in all of the woods. Everything seems to want to grow. Even the non-native florae that has been transported and transplanted into our summer yards or nursed along in our winter homes flourish during these days.

I mentioned earlier that I am a cactophile. I grow about 32 species of cacti. I transplant them out into a rock garden in the summertime and back inside for the winter. Of course the hardy North Dakota cacti (four species) do very well out in the snow and subzero temperatures over winter. And Minnesota has two native species with this hardy nature. It's only the Texas wimps that I have to move in where it's warm and cozy for the winter. But the transplanting is always a pleasant event for me.

I was going to say something about growing; it's about heavy rains on a cactus bed. When we get persistent heavy rains over a period of days, I have a light wooden frame covered with clear plastic that I put over my "pets" to protect them from a too-heavy soaking, even though they are in sandy soil on sloping ground.

However I am convinced that if they could talk, they would say, "Look! You give us precious little water all winter. We are enjoying it, paddling our roots around in some good soaking wet once in a while." And I am convinced that even though they are cacti, they seem to smile and prosper when I neglect to cover them. This matter of growing is always a mystery.

Some insects have taken a liking to my ankles, much to my discomfort. I don't begrudge them, as I expect they are hungry. A little Muskol clears me of their deeds. I see they are a small fly, about half the size of a house fly. I am not much of an entomologist, so their identity escapes me. But they are common and we have seen them many times before.

However I wonder why they take such a liking to my ankles and seem to have no taste for my wrists, neck and everywhere else. Is there something salty and juicy about my ankles that they quite prefer? Ah, now one just took a nip at my elbow and made a liar out of me.

No more nimbus rains. But they have brought heavy winds that make the great trees bend and twist all about me.

Chapter 6: Raspberry Season!

A lone great blue heron stands on the far bank of the river, greeting the morning. He looks not too great at the moment, standing on one leg and bending his head under his wing preening himself, looking more like a twisted tree root. Ah, well, a morning moment while he is at his ablutions is hardly a fair time to judge him. I expect at the first sight of me in the morning mirror, I am not at my best, either.

A beaver enjoys the mid river in the morning sun. He only gave me a moment to notice him before he smacked his tail on the water surface and dove. That is a treat. May I hope that he will show himself again before I leave?

The wheat grass has grown immensely in the last week under the encouragement of some plentiful rains. It is completely headed out, having started already last week. A copse of it stands six feet tall beside me, so impressive that I have abandoned my brown aster stalks and shuttled my woolly lawn chair over and settled into the concealment of the wheat grass.

That move puts me out into the exposure of the morning sun, but a passing of ample cirrus clouds causes the sun to pop in and out of view enough to give me good relief. A touch of coolness makes the morning air just pleasant and inviting.

Out of the corner of my eye to my left, I spot six turkey vultures circling lazily in the sky above. Since I'm an anomaly on this spot, perhaps they're checking out whether I might be a tasty bit of carrion they could enjoy, much to my indignation. Thank you very much, my friends! But now they have given up on me and flown off.

Now a young gray squirrel at the base of a nearby white ash tree is entertaining. He seems to have gone absolutely nuts, if you'll pardon the pun. First he wrestles with a small green plant by the tree. Then he leaps onto the tree trunk, then back onto the plant. Has he found some catnip? Now he grabs a big stick and, rolling onto his back with his white belly showing, he wrestles with it. Quite a show!

While this is going on, a big tom turkey parades by on the far side of the river. He doesn't parade silently; he gives a repeated three gobbles that can be heard up and down the river. I heard him to my right before I saw him. He passed by the heron, who stood alert and watched but seemed otherwise undisturbed. Now I can hear him out of sight far off to my left, still gobbling away. Is everyone into performing this morning? Is he strutting his showy self, looking for a mate?

The day has settled into morning quietness. The beaver has not returned. It was good to see him. He is usually only seen further upriver, rarely here now. But I remember seeing him here many years ago. Perhaps he will return; I will wait and watch for him.

As I wait, I reflect on the nature of this endeavor — this weekly watching, and writing, and reflecting, and learning that has resulted first in weekly newspaper columns and, now, this book.

The happy nature of this endeavor is that it requires so little to enjoy; a Sunday afternoon, a notebook, a pen, a chair and the woods — wherever I am in the world. And yes, to succeed, it helps to think there are readers who care to read what I have to say, and take pleasure in sharing the experience with me.

Being mortal, I know this enterprise cannot go on forever. But what crisis might threaten it? I suppose an illness could suspend the habit; perhaps a term in the hospital or simple inability to visit the woods or nature in the same capacity as I've come to so very much appreciate. Such a crisis would point to a last day of writing, when illness or the infirmities of age dictate the day I must say farewell.

Suppose this is the moment, as I wait for the beaver to return. I cast this cloak of mortality, but for today move out of the shadow of the cloak until I must move under it and close my writing.

*****

The plant growth on the river front is lush and tall now, standing waist-high as you walk through it. I expect it is a product of good rains and no floods this year to tear up the land and leave packed mud flats behind.

I am impressed that in this area of free growth of plants (untilled and unmowed) only a few trees here and there are allowed to succeed. Does all of this smaller plant life dominate the terrain? Surely the large trees scatter thousands of seeds.

A healthy-looking white ash sapling stands about 10 feet in front of me. It looks for all the world as if it is headed for the stature of a mature tree. Yet it is this year's growth. I do not recall it on that spot a year ago. It stands five feet tall now. Will it be gone next year? Will it leave the field to the few big willows, ash, oak and the big old sheltering elm behind me?

A phoebe with its indistinct wing bars interrupts my tree reveries to sport about on the trunk of a dead ash 20 yards ahead. He sits on a branch for a moment in his saucy upright position. I don't catch his traditional tail-wagging. I must try to note that next time, as he has left now.

I realize now that the phoebe-be call (not whistle) I have been hearing and answering is indeed my phoebe friend. I answer and try to get a response but he is very uncooperative and calls back any old time he takes a hankering

It must be that my rendition doesn't sound much like a phoebe. Perhaps it's because I whistle it and he thinks I am a chickadee. What a bunch of dilettantes they think we are.

A black dragonfly hovers near my right elbow, checking me out. He is a lovely creature. But I must not look like a tasty mosquito, for he quickly departs. I remember them off Templar Point on Leech Lake in the evenings, feasting on the day's mosquito supply.

A teal wings by along the river headed north, not 20 feet above the water. As I sit thinking about him, he comes winging back on the same air path, headed south. He always announces his quacking self; can't seem to fly without squawking a bit about it.

A flock of cowbirds grace an open space across the river, a space of very short grass, checking it out for mites and such. They rise as a flock and fly overhead with unaltered even wingbeats.

In a flash of feathers, a female mallard settles down onto the river across from me. She navigates in behind some dead tree branches that are tipped down into the river. Looks as though she might be settled in for the evening.

*****

Raspberry season! My wife gathers the troops, the family, arms us each with a small bucket and marches us off to the berry grounds. The day sports warm sunshine with just a touch of that pleasant northern Minnesota coolness that I love so much.

Now I'm never quite sure about taking off for berry picking as over against just loafing in a lawn chair in the woods under the tall Norway pines, waiting for whatever surprise the woods might offer me that day. As I'm putting on long trousers (one of my kids said to me the other day, "Papa, nobody says they wear 'trousers' anymore today!") and good walking shoes, I wonder why I go through all of this

It's very much like going camping. While packing up the tent, the axe, the food and all the gear, I wonder why I go to all this trouble. Then when I stand by the lake toward evening with a hot, fresh cup of coffee in my hand and watch the sun set over the lake amid the smell of pines, taking in great gulps of unpolluted air with the whip-poor-will beginning his song behind me — I wonder why I wondered why!

Raspberry picking is like that. When I get into the sunny openings in the deep woods with only the quiet hum of the bees on the bluebells and lobelia, and the rosy eye of the ripe, red raspberry nods at me, I wonder why I wondered why.

Now the wink of that raspberry is something else again. First you are looking. Then you spot one. And pretty soon, you discover them all around you, and you are filling your bucket. That rosy eye looks at you as if to say, "Come and take me, I am here for you," very much like Al Capp's shmoo in the Valley of the Shmoon. There is something about the providence in nature that is quite overwhelming and tends to make every day a day of thanksgiving.

Suddenly a grouse explodes out of the brush off the woods path ahead of me. As if waiting for the signal, a startled white tail doe bounds away to my right, only her white tail flag visible to me as she disappears.

Now my wife is the ultimate berry picker, which makes it great fun to go out with her to this berry harvest. But you have to take the rough with the smooth. Just after she announces to all that berry picking is over for the afternoon and we can go home, JoAnn discovers a fresh patch of red, ripe raspberries and says, "No, no. Wait! Wait! We can't go yet. We'll just get these first." And we're off picking again.

However the fresh wild raspberry pies later are worth it. And the raspberries on cereal and in pancakes. And the little row of half pint jars of raspberry jam on the kitchen counter. And the sheer enthusiasm of an avid berry picker.

*****

Half a dozen chipping sparrows move into this tiny spot in the woods, canopied by young white oak trees that bend over me. The sparrows appear to be having a convention here but they are unlike a convention in that they are totally silent.

Some of them approach one another, and I am thinking that they appear to be feeding or attending to young ones. Are the nesting sites for chipping sparrows in places like this?

Suddenly I am visited by one with the identifying black spot or stickpin on his vest that others did not have: a tree sparrow. He is a little noisier, with his tsee-oo.

The forest floor is lush with plant growth after some heavy rains. I see the wild lily of the valley in bloom, a small 4-inch plant that puts forth a white cluster blossom in the very shady woods. I wonder if it is blossoming late, as the season is late this year.

Folks who arrived here May 1 said the ice was solid on the lake then. A week later it was beginning to disappear. Some very warm weather helped the warming of the lake. Today, less than two months later, it is very pleasant for swimming. Nature rushes into action when the weather is tardy.

The evening settles in. The first frog sounds off to my left. A sky that had been clouded with rain is almost clear blue now; only a few fleecy cumulus clouds peek between the tall Norway pines.

Although it is evening, it appears to be almost like daytime, being nearly the longest day of the year. After a very long winter, we northerners relish the respite of these pleasant solstice evenings.

The bullfrogs have become a chorus now. The first whippoorwill sounds off surprisingly; he is a little early for his nighttime serenades. Perhaps he wants to lengthen the short nights a bit.

*****

A great blue heron sails in suddenly from my right, passes by and lands 150 yards downstream. I rarely see him along here. Very likely the still partly-flooded Red River gives him plenty of shallow over-the-bank water in which to wade.

I notice he landed in a copse of green ash sprouts that have sprung up and grown tall from an old ash stump on the river bank. So I decide to go closer to see if I can get a good look — stalk him, so to speak. I figure he has landed on the far side of the ash copse, out of sight. That should enable me to get quite close before he discovers me.

At Home in the Woodlands

Then I see something stark white ahead of me, in front of the copse, something that shouldn't be there; so it must be the heron. I eye him with the glasses and see he has already discovered this human stalker trying to sneak up on him.

I had forgotten that, except for a caballero dash of black feathers tracing back from his eyebrows, this heron has a starkly-white head, hardly fitting camouflage for otherwise-splendid coloration for blending into his background.

He eyed me without alarm. Then he flew off casually and landed a short distance upstream, out of sight.

Several turkey vultures sail leisurely by, headed upstream into the wind. Their black underparts offer no variation in coloration. Their method of soaring identifies them. The experts call the method of holding their wings by the term "dihedral," a fancy word that means "swooped-up," instead of flat like the eagle.

The presence of vultures and herons offers interesting questions about why they are here. The river has flooded because of heavy rains upriver. Two weeks ago, I would have been up to my chin in water where I am sitting now. I am wondering: Does flooding dredge up food that these birds seek?

A red-winged blackbird serenades me from the tall grass and willow shoots along the river bank, but he refuses to reveal himself. He gives a very summery feeling to the day.

The small fly I noted several weeks ago persists in tasting me. Several people from gardens and strolls this week have remarked how these fellows have made themselves known to them. This fly must have hatched out in early June and is complimenting us by indicating we make a tasty meal. Again, a little Muskol helps keep them a little distance from me. A good stiff breeze keeps this summer afternoon very pleasant.

A white cabbage butterfly flits across the tops of the grasses directly in front of me, belying the animal inactivity on this hot, hot 90-degree afternoon. He does not seem intent upon leaving and obviously loves the sun and doesn't mind the heat. Will he be here to entertain me when I come to the end of my time here this afternoon?

No, no, I lied about the inactivity. Three goldfinches have darted into the top of the tall willow on the riverbank 20 yards in front of me, flashing their bright yellow breasts in the summer sun. They've joined the butterfly. It seems that creatures with light colors that reflect the sun's heat are handling this heat the best

A tall willow on the river bank continues to amaze me. It must get battered terribly by the ice when the river comes even a little out of its banks in the spring. Yet it survives and does the service of holding the river bank at that place. Seven slender white ash trees that are almost as tall as that prairie willow have given up the ghost and only stand as tall stalks of their former selves. Yet they, too, help to hold the river bank in their own way. All of these, ash and willow alike, lean rakishly north in the direction of the flow of the river water and ice. I am grateful that no obsessive clean-niks feel driven to cut down these dead stalks to improve the look of the riverfront.

At Home in the Woodlands

An almost totally blue sky greeted me as I came here today. A few fleecy cumulus clouds hovered at the tree line south of me, lazily drifting north. It is only by their juxtaposition to the tree tops that I can get any sense of their movement.

If these clouds were cooperative enough to retain their shape, I might be able to track their progress across the sky space, almost 180 degrees, in front of me. But that cloud that looks like a sleeping caterpillar now would likely resemble an overfed buffalo later on. Also their pace is not cooperatively consistent. One moment they seem to be tripping along at a good rate, and then they appear to have stalled altogether. They are an agony to rate-watchers.

I mentioned before the new green ash 20 feet in front of me. It has now reached a healthy six feet and its top leaves look me in the eye. Will this ash last until next summer, or will the ice slice it down next spring? Is the hope for its future dependent on some floodless years that will enable it to grow strong enough to withstand that punishment?

But it cannot be as simple as that. This 35-yard wide strip of riparian area sports only a random large tree here and there and is otherwise dominated by the grasses. I would have to explore this matter further to understand this.

Another winged visitor comes. He sits like a phoebe, but I see a flash of yellow on his back as he ducks down under the brush. Is he one of the flycatchers? I won't know today, I guess.

The cabbage butterfly visited me once more but then not again. Even he has retired due to the heat.

*****

In what strange fashion has the land become a lake! Four inches of rain in one night, and much more upriver, have driven the Red River over its banks and almost to a stage that resembles the spring floods.

The river has begun to ebb so that I am able to sit where I would have been over my ankles in water a week ago. Some warm weather has quickly dried the surface of the land so it's suitable for comfortable walking. I've placed a marker to see if it will recede more during the time I am here.

On hard surfaces that are still damp with a very thin layer of mud, small worms snake their way under the surface, tracing vine-like patterns in the mud. They are invisible, but I can mark their progress at the head of each pattern, as the sun sparkles on their forms and betrays their progress.

Now the ground feeders move in at the edge of the receding water; the robin, for example, who is the stuff of legend with his persistent tug at stubborn worms who refuse to come out of the ground. Now I see the grackles join them, fussing about in the grass for food. But worms? I had not known this would be on their diet. I connect a grackle with eating a farmer's corn. So I watch and, sure enough, I see one pick up a big earthworm. Now he bends down and puts his foot on one end of the worm. Pulling up with his beak, he proceeds to tear it to pieces. He seems to know what to do with a worm.

Now another sight unfolds. Several nuthatches move onto a big white oak a dozen feet in front of me. Nuthatches are always great fun to watch for their upside-down antics on tree trunks, but now they offer me a special treat. One peers into a hole in the side of the tree, where a six-inch thick branch has broken off. I never have known where they live in the woods and hold my breath to see if he will go in. But he teases me. He moves away and proceeds to search for lunch under some bark. However, a few moments later he returns as I watch and disappears into the hole: his home. Does he have a brood in there?

Soon a small sparrow flies into the short grass about 20 feet in front of me and begins hopping about nervously in search of lunch, giving me a good chance to look at him. He has a white eye line and rusty cap, but he lacks the wing bars of the chipping sparrow and the yellow beak of the field sparrow. I am looking at the swamp sparrow, who has apparently declared our riverfront a swamp for the day. I have only seen him in July in past years. He normally likes only brackish swamps and cattails. He is a very nervous, busy little fellow.

A pileated woodpecker flies in. He whacks away at a couple of trees, and then flies off.

I check my marker. The water has receded nearly a full inch since I have been here. So it is gradually returning to its lazy river form.

*****

I leave the river to its recession as I return to the less volatile expanse of Ham Lake. Oh, the lakes too have their volatility and storms and such, but in this part of the world, the profile of the lake in the woods remains pretty much the same after a violent storm as before.

I am given pause to realize that I am not like the lake. If you beat me about too brutally, the profile of the spirit within me will change. I may even be prevented from going on as I did before.

What would it take to alter this journey I am making into the ongoing aura of the woods? An illness or injury so violent that it would demand my physical and/or psychological resources to recover? Death would do it, of course. But for now, while I'm healthy, on with my journey.

*****

A yellowjacket lands near me. He ambles about a bit, then settles himself and sits still. He seems intent upon outlasting me by not allowing me to see him move again.

A slow rain has settled upon the forest, one of those good all-day rains that the thirsty forest gladly drinks up for the life-sustaining moisture it needs. Perhaps the yellowjacket has found a bit of shelter in the foliage and is content to wait out of the rain.

Most of the forest life has followed suit and found some cozy shelter out of the wet here at Ham Lake. Tomorrow is soon enough to go about their business.

An exception is a band of crows that has flown down onto the forest floor in a little open glen in the middle of the woods, pecking the ground cover, searching for lunch of some kind — a very uncrow-like activity in the middle of the rain. I have never seen a group of crows before on the ground in that little glen. What are they after? Has something just hatched out? Why in the rain? And why crows, instead of some other birds?

If it were a city lawn, I would expect to see robins out there, extracting earthworms. But there are no earthworms here in this sand with a bare cover of pine needles.

How still the forest seems in this very, very gentle rain. The only movement is an occasional raindrop hitting some single leaf among the foliage and causing it to dance. The only sound is the intermittent patter of rain on bark or branch nearby. It is as if the forest has given over the day to this lord of moisture and life-giving drink and will not compete with any sound or movement.

I am sitting in an elevated place today. This is not a deer stand but it would remind one of such a place. I look out over the top of the ground foliage that stretches up eight or 10 feet above the forest floor — alder, hackberry and the like. The foliage top is like a sea of green that undulates out from me in all directions. The giant Norway pines reach above me.

The life of birds in the rain is interesting. Their experiences must be extremely varied. A mother phoebe sits on her nest, but she has provided her young with shelter under the eaves of a building. I have seen the house finch — and sometimes the robin — do the same.

But what of the ospreys that build nests in places such as the tops of towering dead pines? There is only the parent's body to protect the chicks from pounding, drenching rainstorms. And indeed, all open nests in the forest are the same. The wild creatures tolerate the rain, and when it is over, shake their feathers or fur, and go on.

A mosquito lands on my arm and ambles about, checking me out to see if I offer possibilities for an evening meal, just as I'm settling comfortably into my chair in the deep woods by Ham Lake. He stabs me. I squash him.

After a fair interval, another drops by and checks me out. Stab. Squash.

What do I do? Rush off frantically and lather myself up good with repellent? Or live with them?

I opt to live with them, understanding that when my body cools down from the exercise I expended coming to this spot, they won't find me anyway. At least they haven't (bless their little hearts) insulted me by checking me out and leaving because I didn't taste good.

A downy woodpecker lands on a small dead branch of a very tall Norway pine about 25 feet in front. He does not engage in his usual pecking, which I expect, but instead begins to industriously preen himself.

He makes a general mess, fluffing his feathers out in all directions, rather like my hair sometimes looks in the morning mirror. However he seems to be enjoying himself thoroughly, prancing about on the branch as he preens, so I certainly don't begrudge him his good time. And it does seem rather like he is sprucing up for an evening date.

The undergrowth in the deep woods intrigues me. I wonder what makes certain plants grow. A year ago I traced the progress of a raspberry plant on this spot, through the course of the summer — which was a bust. In the deep

At Home in the Woodlands

woods, away from the hot sun, is obviously not a place where a raspberry will prosper.

This year I am looking at a small elm to see how it prospers. It is 10 inches tall at the moment and looks very healthy.

It lives under a small white oak about eight feet tall, which lives under a towering Norway that reaches up 80 feet into the sky. So it has some competition.

It is interesting how these forests change with time. I am privileged to experience only one stage in its development, because my life span is so short, compared to that of the forest.

I see the poplars and birches and know they were the first stage that sprang up when this forest was new growth — after a fire, logging or what? They were dominant at one time.

Now the great pines have reached high above them. When I have arrived, this second stage is what I experience. I might hastily conclude that this is the ultimate stage. However a forestry department film at Itasca Park years ago informed me that these oaks and maples that nestle today at the feet of tall pines will one day, years from now, reach up and dominate the pine forest long after I am dead and buried, and my grandchildren will see that.

A lone mosquito buzzes about my ear but does not land. They have allowed me the peace of my forest time.

A hairy woodpecker greets me with his two-note chortle. I can trace his movements across the forest in front of me, but he refuses to let himself be seen. Finally his call dies away to the north. Will he return to entertain me before I leave?

A hot, hot day settles upon the woods, under a clear blue, totally cloudless sky. Only the quaking aspen twirls its leaves a little under the slightest breeze issuing up from the lake, 100 yards behind me.

There! My friend, the hairy, has returned. I hear him now out of sight behind me.

I am always curious about what kind of growth change takes place in a given spot in the woods from week to week. I know it is constant, but how stealthy it is, and how easy it would be for a human to conclude that nothing changes from week to week. The only comment to the contrary that I've heard humans make is that on hot, sultry nights in Iowa, you can hear corn grow.

The 10-inch elm that I observed here in the deep woods a week ago has changed not at all. Perhaps in this deeply-shaded forest he has done all he will do for this year. He has sprouted and grown his few leaves and he will remain alive for another year.

A lone white cumulus cloud appears in front of me in the blue sky at about a 40-degree angle from me. Where did he come from? There are no others in the sky.

Then, amazing! I watch him totally evaporate; disappear before my very eyes, leaving only the blue sky again and the memory of the cloud. I had not expected that.

At Home in the Woodlands

What did I expect? It would seem that we humans piece together bits of information to fill in the gaps for what we do not understand. We are uncomfortable without some kind of closure in this regard. Where there is no sense, we want somehow to make sense out of it.

Very likely I expected a small cloud like this would drift into a great bank of clouds somewhere beyond my vision and be absorbed into it. But to just vanish before my very eyes! Does that mean that if I were to gaze patiently and steadily at a piece of blue sky, I could see a cloud materialize before my very eyes?

To the left of me, an 18-inch berry plant, with five bright red berries on it, graces the forest floor. I will watch it in the future, but I expect since it has flowered, fruited and produced seed, this is all it will do for this season. We commonly call this plant the bunchberry.

My friend the hairy came and went once more but without showing himself. He seems to say it is too hot today for such performances.

I had some reservations about coming out into the deep woods in a red cap. Hardly the costume for camouflage.

And sure enough, within a half hour, a ruby-throated hummingbird hummed in to check me out. But when I didn't act or smell like a bright red peony, he departed.

A sky overcast with strato-cumulus clouds has now broken up into soft fleecy cumulous ones and now offers great patches of bright blue summer sky. We have a pleasant summer day.

The veery entertains me from a distance with his down-sliding single musical note, but he refuses to let himself be seen. He seems to like to begin his serenading in the woods late in the day.

The lowly mosquito (and his companions) settles in on me to check me out for tastiness. I am protected, so he doesn't bother me. He flits about here and there, looking for an unprotected spot. When I first arrive I have exercised a bit and am putting out heat, which attracts him. After a while, my body cools to the temperature of the air around me, and his heat-seeking devices no longer discover me and, as Mark Twain puts it, he "pretty much" can't find me anymore. So here I sit; a tasty meal and no one to eat me.

I remember in younger years sleeping outdoors with some buddies in the summertime without a tent, and the mosquitoes would visit us. As we tried to get to sleep in our sleeping bags, we debated how many hours it would take for mosquitoes to entirely drain us dry of blood on a good mosquito night like we were experiencing.

Of course we had the hoods of the sleeping bags pulled up over our heads so that only our faces were showing. With our sleeping bags warming our bodies, we were pumping out buckets of heat from that little face hole, so that critters with heat-seeking devices had a heyday finding us. Needless to stay, we're still here, making more blood.

A blue jay calls over to my left but out of sight. I haven't yet seen him this summer, but he is announcing his presence.

A persistent breeze sways the tops of the noble giant Norway pines, though it seems very still here on the forest floor.

At Home in the Woodlands

These giants amaze me. With the hard substance of their woody trunks, these trunks are still flexible enough to allow the tops of the trees to sway many feet from side to side in a violent wind and not snap off. These fibrous trunks boast a remarkable substance in their makeup.

The soughing of the wind continues but begins gradually to abate as the day proceeds. It is as if the soughing musician is dancing farther and farther away.

A kingfisher darts across the opening in the Norway pines by the lakefront, heading for a new fish-watching post. There is always something business-like about the kingfisher.

It occurs to me that I have only actually seen a kingfisher fishing once. He dove into the water like a bullet. I saw a small splash. A moment later, he rose from the water with a small fish in his beak. He flew up into the trees and disappeared.

The other day I saw four of them together, darting along the shore of Ham Lake from perch to perch. They seem to spend most of their time darting. I suppose this is the way they do their fish-hunting.

A midsummer peace has settled over the woods. A slight breeze sways the tops of a giant Norway pine that towers perhaps 65 feet above me. Comparing the size of the Norway's trunk at its base with some other cut logs in the area, the tree is perhaps 60 years old. That means it hadn't quite started when the first cabins were built along this side of the lake, but the tree was about to seed and sprout very soon. It could have observed and recorded the entire history of this spot during that period. It quietly marks time, while we move about beneath it.

I am always awed by the strength of these stout trees, truly the top of the chain of botanical life. I have seen the tops of these trees sway five or six feet in a stiff wind, and yet the apparently rock-hard wood of their great trunks flexes without breaking.

Small mosquitoes move in with me as I settle here in the woods. But I do not begrudge them finding me tasty for a little time. After a short while, they lose interest in me and leave me in peace. A few of them bite the dust from my swatting (they are easy targets). One limps away across my board with a broken wing.

The mass of plant growth on the forest floor in the deep woods is overwhelming. I'm sure the number of species here is not in the thousands but it must at least be in the hundreds.

To consider such things in the woods is like one of Kant's antinomies: to consider the thickness of the filament in the web of the tiniest spider is too small for the human mind; to consider the number of species in the thick undergrowth of the forest floor in the deep woods is too great for the human mind. Perhaps I must look at a tiny eight-inch square spot on the forest floor and consider that for another time.

*****

As I settle in again along the Red River, several bats sail about among some white ash trees across the river from me, and I am able to pick them up in my glasses and follow them about for a few minutes. They are an unusual sight.

What brings them out? Is it the approaching evening? Is it the blossoming among some of the riparian plants, and are they feasting on the nectar? The Canadian thistle is blossoming this week with their beautiful big lavender blossoms. Or is it the evening mosquitos that bring them out?

I know so little about bats. Is this what they call the brown bat? It flashes a lighter color as it wheels about in the sun, but that may only be the sunlight on it.

The tall grass around the spot where I sit, some of it five feet tall, has headed out and turned brown. It is a hearty growth, appearing in patches each 30 square feet or so, here and there along the riparian area.

My Iowa mentor, David Osheim, informs me that it is the reed canary grass. It can grow in the partial shade of oak woodlands, which is what we have here, but we also have some of it in the fertile moist organic soil here in the full sun, which is what it likes best.

I learn that it is an aggressive intrusive species, and folks try to get rid of it. We attack it with herbicides, but it tends to persevere. David tells me we have some success with glyphosate, but despite our best efforts, reed canary grass will still be here long after we are gone. It's a humbling thought.

A lone house fly lands on my notebook and entertains me. He flits out onto the open writing board. He faces me and holds still for several moments as if checking me out for any threat. After this pause he decides I'm OK and this sun-warmed board is a good spot to relax and preen.

First he balances on his front four legs and with his two hind legs proceeds to brush his hindquarters. Next, with those same two legs he brushes and brushes the undersides of his wings. That completed, he brushes his two front legs together. I whistle at a nearby bird and watch for his reaction. Nothing. He keeps preening. Hmmm. Does he not have hearing?

A half moon rises above the tree line of the ash trees across the river into an almost clear blue sky. I say almost, because to the left of the moon some cirro-cumulus clouds gather, looking like the patterned tufts of a chenille bedspread. They were pure white, but now they are gathering a rose hue from the sun, which has just set behind me.

Gradually the moon rises on a 45-degree path as it proceeds on its ecliptic march in an arc through the night sky, following the sun, until it disappears at the sun-setting spot on the western rim of the earth. For another night, tonight, it will illuminate this arc in the sky, as it continues its old, old journey around our planet.

I've watched for them, but the bats have not returned as I'd hoped they might. They considered it enough to simply announce the evening and then be on their way.

*****

A Canada jay greets me from the branches of a black spruce, here at the end of the Gunflint Trail in northeastern

Minnesota, where I find myself this morning. He eyes me, cocks his head, and then looks away, as if bored by my presence.

He's obviously accustomed to these two-legged mortals in hiking boots who inhabit his woods in the fair weather season that these pansies prefer. These mortals are occasionally bothersome, but they are good for free lunches, if a jay keeps his eye peeled for an unguarded food item left on a picnic table. We recall visiting here in the early 1960s when a jay landed on the head of our infant son, Doug, to check out our camp. Doug was mostly indignant that he was being used as a perch.

As I settled into my woolly chair, an ovenbird greets me from another spruce. As I watch her, I discover she isn't greeting me at all but dealing with an obstreperous youngster that is demanding breakfast in no uncertain terms. It is he who is making most of the ruckus, and she is calling back in her distinctive beautiful eight-note whistle. "Keep your shirt on," she calls back sweetly, as she hunts frantically for food. He's easily big enough to do his own hunting. She hunts for something in a big old dead spruce nearby and brings it to him.

How different and demanding he is from sweet, gentle, undemanding human infants who don't even complain when birds perch on their heads.

How absolutely amazing these great granite rocks are in this Canadian Shield country. I sit on top of one perhaps 80 feet above beautiful Seagull Lake that shimmers in the morning sun below. This is actually only a small arm of this huge lake, an arm that stretches 200 yards across to a spruce, pine and cedar forested area on another big rock on the other side (probably an extension of the same rock I'm sitting on).

Outcroppings of this rock appear all around, interspersed by the forest growing on it. The rocks are worn smooth now by wind and weather, so unlike, I can imagine their rough, jagged appearance 50 million years ago, when they were infants like the ovenbird and lay naked of any forest clothing.

A herring gull sails across the breadth of my view, from right to left, seeming to find it unnecessary to expend any energy flying but simply floating on the wings of the wind. He disappears to the north and heads for the big lake.

A chickadee rewards me with a visit on the lower branches of a tall white cedar 10 feet in front of me. He nods in my direction, and then busies himself worrying the new cones on the cedar. He had announced his presence a few minutes before with his familiar call of "pip-pip."

The jays continue to sport about among the spruces. "Whiskey jacks," my dad and his friends used to call them when they hunted up north. They were here to greet him and now me. And one day they will greet my great-great-grandchildren up here.

*****

The morning sun just tops the skyline of the Norway pines as I settle into the woods back at Ham Lake. Its rise is directly in front of me, brilliantly backlighting all of the woods flora before me.

At Home in the Woodlands

The downside of such a sunrise is that I have a very much "in your face" sun. The upside, however, is that it shimmers all of the hundreds (thousands?) of spider webs that network the woods; which, without the sun's backlighting, are invisible to the human eye.

It makes me realize that as I make my first walk through such a morning woods, I collect a network of webs upon my person. Yet the spiders quickly re-spin them.

A small bird appears on a log to my right, then quickly darts behind some foliage, eluding identification. He appears to be about wren-size and I have seen the wren in the area in the past few days. Now, out of sight, he treats me to his song, the familiar rise and fall of the song of the house wren.

Now to my left, another small bird is working the lower foliage for bugs and such. I catch yellow markings on it, but it moves out of view too quickly to allow me a good look at it. It appears to have the markings of the female redstart. I have not seen the redstart in these parts for a number of years. But they do seem to like the deep woods, as I recall.

The abundance of plant species on the forest floor continues to amaze me. I would think their identification would be a definite challenge to the botanist.

I have selected a spot eight inches square for my small-botanist mind to observe. Four separate species live together in that tiny square alone. One is a grass. A second is a five-leafed ivy. A third has a small plantain-type leaf. The fourth has the look of an hepatica. They have been well-watered by the rains in the last few days. It will be interesting to see how they prosper together.

*****

A small patch of fleecy cumulus clouds moves lazily across an opening in the Norway pines in an otherwise mostly blue sky on this quiet summer afternoon. It transforms itself into a ghostly shroud, and then mischievously disappears behind the trees.

How cannily the forest forms itself into as ring around you, when you place yourself in a single spot for a while. It is very like one's poetic description of a "circle of friends" to describe close acquaintances. One can hardly describe their human configuration as a circle, but in one's imagination they seem to form a comforting circle around a person.

A similar experience seems to happen in a spot one has chosen in the deep woods. Here to the left is the slender trunk of a small white oak. There to the right is the 22-inch bole of a towering Norway pine. Straight ahead is a graceful cluster of maiden hair ferns. Behind is a cluster of alder completing the circle. They would hardly describe a circle, but for the moment you are their center, and they are your woodland friends.

One is intensely aware of this if one sits by a small campfire in the midst of the deep woods in the dead of night. The campfire light seems to cast a definable light on the trees around you.

These trees form a perfect circle about you, exactly at the distance the little campfire is able to cast its light in every direction over 360 degrees. They stand as comforting sentinels that seem to say you are safe within that circle.

And if large animals would hesitate to approach a fire, in a sense that safety is true. And as light would tend to guide your steps, you could walk safely within that circle, but less safely outside of that circle in the darkness.

As you look straight upward from your campfire the trees form a column of shelter, its top spilling out into the stars above you. You are in a small woods home.

A single crow flies into the top of this woodland column and lands in the top of a tall poplar tree perhaps 60 feet above me. He caws a time or two, and then flies off. A half hour later another single crow flies in and does the same. This has usually happened in times past when I have settled into this spot. I can't help feeling, since they land so close by me, that they are aware of my presence. It is as if they are self-appointed sentinels sent to check out this aberration on the forest floor. Then, finding me no apparent threat, they fly off and make no more fuss.

Gradually the afternoon wanes, leaving a totally blue sky, without a shred of a cloud in sight.

A hairy woodpecker chitters away to my right. A small bee hovers by a tiny blossom nearby.

The woods have grown very still. A mourning dove coos in the distance.

*****

We visit Lamoure, North Dakota, for the 125th anniversary of St. Ansgar, a picturesque old country church that I knew half a century ago. A little stream ten miles south of town runs through a little valley, providing trees by the stream that I figure could be my "woods" this time.

Tearing myself away from the festivities, I set up my wooly brown chair under the shade of some massive prairie willows and settle in to enjoy the serenity of this place. Actually this spot is by the little stream's backwaters, so the water is not flowing; but I'm content.

So I shall call this spot a pond rather than a stream. I am surrounded by a healthy stand of brome grass three feet tall. The pond is half-filled with cattail rushes. The water comes from a little draw 50 yards in front of me through which flows the little stream.

A winged visitor serenades me immediately. He gives a distinctive eight-note call, all on one pitch: 1-2/1-2-3-4-5/si-i-i-ix. I don't recognize it. Then he presents himself 15 feet in front of me on an old willow branch. He is back-lit (my excuse), so that I can't identify him. What is he? He is thrush-size. He dances down among the cattails after something, and then finally disappears. He even answers me.

Two kingbirds present themselves on an old willow tree 80 yards in front of me. They sit out majestically and unapologetically like the "kings" that they are, on the topmost branches of the tree, searching the area for passing insects.

Several vesper sparrows dash in among the tall brome grass. They cavort about with each other for a few moments and then dive down into the tall grass, out of sight, after some lunch.

Half a dozen black butterflies flit about on the grass tops. Apparently something is in bloom on which they are feeding. They move about, coming quite close at times. I must learn to identify them. I miss the monarchs, which used to be plentiful and which I rarely see anymore.

Now a viceroy butterfly comes close and capers around for a bit. He is as close to a monarch as I am going to see.

The memory lingers of this place. I recall coming out to this little church 50 years ago, where there were no telephones to disturb me. I came to find a quiet place to read and study. In those days, little country churches were not locked and were there for one to come in for a bit of quiet meditation.

I remember in early spring, when there was still snow on the ground, I would see this little stream break through its ice and begin to flow briskly through the snow; the first spring freshet. One could hear it before you saw it.

I thought then it would be fun to come back sometime and sit beside this freshet and enjoy it in summer weather.

It has taken me half a century to fulfill that dream.

*****

A loon wails his lonely evening call from Ham Lake 100 yards behind me. A moment later, he breaks into his bright-toned laugh. Then abruptly he settles back into his wail to announce the evening. Now he is silent. Perhaps he will serenade me again before I leave.

A small oak 12 feet tall arches over where I sit. His trunk is barely three inches thick at its base and his topmost leaves bend back halfway to the ground to my left. He is healthy, but why is he bent like an old man, rather than reaching straight and tall toward the sun? A great poplar has fallen nearby. Did some of its branches pin the small oak to the ground when it was young?

A small spider spins down from the young oak, which arches over me. He descends almost to my writing board, pauses above my green writing pen as if deciding what to do next. Then he clambers back up, apparently figuring my pen won't do for an attachment for his web. He swings off in an alternate direction.

The amazing part of it all is that the web he spins remains invisible to the eye. He seems to climb on unseen strands of air. When I rise, my face will, no doubt, pass through his gossamer web, and I will walk away with it trailing form my skin. He is beginning his night's work. On mornings I have felt those webs across narrow woodland paths.

A hairy woodpecker sounds his chut-chut as he pecks away on some poplar bark behind me. He is mostly out of sight to me. He has such strange table manners; he can't seem to dine without talking as he eats.

The little 10-inch elm that I have been watching here in the woods has not seemed to change much. He has every disadvantage here in the shade of the forest. But this week he has put out two tiny fresh light green new leaves, as if to say he is not quite through for the season. I say "disadvantage," but he does have the advantage of a forest floor that does not dry out on these hot August weeks. I do not see tall elms about. Whence comes his seed?

A miniature mosquito lands and checks me out, then flies off, insulting me that he will not stay for dinner. I should warn him he should watch out for the spider webs overhead, or he will become dinner for a hungry spider.

Gradually the evening settles down around me in the forest. The evening is mostly quiet. A pleasant evening coolness gathers with the approaching night. The single whistle of a thrush comes from in front of me, but out of sight. The loons do not call again. Even they seem to have settled down for the evening. But I know they can waken in the night and wail and laugh enough to spook a greenhorn camper.

*****

A creeping bellflower greets me as I settle into the deep woods today. It lifts its elegant stalk of multiple violet blooms above the ferns surrounding it, 20 feet in front of me.

I am told it is much more plentiful, even along the roadsides, in other years than it is this year. I was surprised to see it in the deep woods, but I see a narrow, clear shaft of space reaching up above it through the tall poplars to the open sky, offering it a spell of sunshine each day. I am also told that people even cultivate this flower in their gardens for its bold and beautiful blossoms. It offers a pleasant color surprise amidst the pervasive green of the forest floor

A small brown moth no bigger than a copper penny flutters by and lands within my reach among some brown leaves on the forest floor. I am at a loss to discover him there, as he is so perfectly camouflaged. I only know he is there because I had seen him move to that spot.

Wondering if I had imagined his flight, I reach toward the spot where I saw him land. He takes flight but flies only a few feet, still landing within my reach.

Again I am at a loss to detect him with my eyes. I reach for him, and he moves once more, but again only a few feet. It is as if he knows his best protection is not flight but camouflage. It would seem that even a bird that wanted him for lunch would have difficulty finding him.

Now I am suddenly treated to the arrival of a red-eyed vireo 10 feet in front of me, foraging among the leaves of an alder bush. He reaches for some morsel and enables me to see a very faint trace of yellow on his breast.

I wanted to lift my glass and study him a bit, but he is much too busy to allow for that and flits off into the bushes. He makes several stops but keeps moving on until he is out of sight. I obviously must keep my binoculars handier if I am to study a busy vireo. He is not going to sit in one place and preen himself for my benefit when he is on the foraging trail.

It was quite a thrill to see this vireo. I had not had a chance to see him at work before in the underbrush.

Peterson, the bird man, tells us that both warblers and vireos work the underbrush like this, but warblers are much more agile and expert at flitting about among the leaves. Vireos tend to be more sluggish in their movements. Well, I can't say as to that. I didn't have the two of them flitting side by side to make a flit-check.

A fair wind stirs the branches of the trees about me. A beautiful giant birch in front of me reaches up and dusts the sky with its twinkling leaves. Fleecy cumulus clouds move across the sky at a fair pace. It would appear that we will have a change in the weather before tomorrow.

After an hour, a gray-cheeked thrush lands on the forest floor about eight feet in front of me. He dances forward to six feet, apparently finding me an unobjectionable part of the terrain as long as I don't move. I seem to recall that most small birds have fairly poor eyesight for distinguishing something unusual in the terrain, but they quickly detect movement, especially if accompanied by sound.

After a moment the little thrush begins dancing in a circle around to my left, stopping momentarily to peck at something on the ground in an experimental sort of way to see if it might be tasty. Apparently I appeared to be something like a formidable barn wall in the woods that he couldn't dance right through.

When he was four feet to my left I had a good chance to study him, although I didn't dare raise my glasses for a good look. He sported a fairly-evident eye ring and pronounced streaking on his breast, and the gray back. He looked so small, I estimated perhaps eight inches, that I thought he must be a juvenile. But I discovered eight inches is the full growth of this thrush.

I sit in a spot entirely surrounded by alder bushes and a stand of young poplars, the alders almost touching me. I found it a bit of a challenge to push through the thicket and was surprised to come upon this small open spot. Then I discovered deer scat at my feet and realized other visitors frequent this spot, perhaps to rest here and help to enlarge the little opening.

I'm only beginning to realize that almost all plants in the forest flower, fruit and seed. The botanist would no doubt say, "Duh! Who doesn't know that?" But if I am typical of us novices, we usually don't connect the three. We are mostly aware of flowers and pollinating. As an example, I see the hummingbird at work now in a tiny sunlit flower-bearing opening to my left.

At the base of every flower is the fruit, and inside every fruit is the seed. It is all magnificently designed to prolong the species. I looked at the five-leafed ivy all around me at my feet, for example; a splendid little woodland plant that never grows more than two feet tall. And although I realize it increases by runners extending under the forest floor, still I puzzle as to where is the flower and the fruit and the seed to prolong its species? It must produce its fruit and seed at the confluence of the five leaves, produce some kind of berry and drop off long before this point in the summer; even as I've observed poison ivy produce berries.

I must observe this pervasive little plant earlier in the season next year. Nature never tires of teaching us.

*****

The soughing of a zephyr breeze in the tops of the tall Norway pines is all that greets me as I settle into the deep woods today. All animal life seems to be at rest. Will even the breeze diminish as the evening progresses?

I have in front of me a slice of the trunk of a dead jackpine cut down over here near the shore of Ham Lake. Its ring count is 26, marking its age. The trunk is eight inches in diameter.

Using a simple formula (for example, a 16-inch pine would be 52 years old), I became curious about the age of the big trees in this small piece of woods. I always wonder about the sameness and different qualities of a piece of forest over time.

I feel that we humans make the mental adjustment of saying, "This piece of forest is the same as when I last visited it." Of course, in our heart of hearts, we know that nothing here is the same as when we last visited. But that is an example of one of Kant's antinomies: Such an idea is too large for our minds to grasp.

So we settle for the notion, "It is the same." That fallen poplar tree yonder is the same as when I was last here. This young oak arching over me is the same. That 58-year-old Norway pine to my left that I just measured is the same as when I last saw it. The two-foot alder in front of me is the same as when I last saw it. That blue sky up above is the same.

We would like the forest to be like our house at home. When we come home from work at night and approach our front door, we expect our house to be the same as when we left in the morning. When we come to a same spot in the forest, it is comfortable to think it is the same as when we last saw it.

(Of course, if we lived in the torrid equatorial jungles where changes happen almost hourly, we might think differently than we northerners.)

After finding the slice of jack pine, I measured a big old Norway pine down by the lake front, the biggest in the area — and, sadly, one that is dying. It would be 61 years and nine months old. It was a mere one-year-old seedling the year before my family thought about settling here.

That means when I first visited here in 1948 and sat on a spot about 200 yards from where I am sitting now, nothing - nothing was here that is here now. That is awesome to consider. And yet, by casual observation, I would look at the spot and say it looks about the same as it did then.

What puzzles me is that on Templar Point, where we camped in summers for 45 years, there still stand a big old white pine and a big old cottonwood that seem to look about the same as when we first came. I'm sure they are not, but we have trouble getting our minds around changes that are so slow.

The soughing of the wind has settled down to complete silence now, preparing for the quiet of the evening. One hears the evening chirping of frogs from wet places nearby.

*****

It's early morning. Can I spot the place on the horizon where the sun will rise? Gradually that place moves south as summer wanes and September is upon us at Ham Lake.

The sky is completely covered this morning with an overcast of strato-cumulus clouds. Only a slight brightening of the horizon at the spot where the sun will appear betrays that sunrise.

The woods seem entirely quiet this morning, except for a breeze stirring the poplar leaves above me and the sigh of the wind in the great Norway pines. It seems these woods are relaxing into the end of summer.

Suddenly I catch the movement of a single dark bird to my left at about eye level. He moves up to the trunk of a nearby pine; a hairy woodpecker. He is the first visitor to greet me on this quiet morning, as he sets out in search of his breakfast.

A loon sends out his mournful wail from the direction of another lake to my left, to remind me that he is also up for the morning. An answering loon call from Ham Lake behind me completes the loon chorus.

I hear the three-note song of a single bird at a distance ahead of me. It sounds like the piping of a thrush, but he will not come nearer for me to see him.

Earlier in the summer I remarked on the plethora of plant species on the forest floor around me, too much for one to get one's mind around. It makes me realize what a beginner I am at getting to know all of the low-growing flora that surround me in just this one spot in the woods. It is as if nature went berserk in developing new and different species for this one place on the globe.

At that time I selected an eight-inch spot on the forest floor near where I sit, defined its outline in an unobtrusive way and have watched it from week to week. It contained four plants — a grass, an ivy, an arrow plant and a hepatica.

The four plants remained mostly unchanged over the weeks, having apparently reached their mature growth before I first observed them. In the last week or two, the arrow plant has disappeared, seemingly having completed its labors for this year and retired to rest until it reappears to do its work next summer.

Late summer rains have kept the flora on the forest floor looking freshly green. Only slim traces of browning on a few leaves suggest the coming of autumn.

The hour suggests the sun has already risen and slipped up into the sky behind its cover of overcast, that rascal. I shall have to wait to view the sunrise on a sunnier day and call it a morning for now.

Chapter 7: End of a Perfect Day

"When you come to the end of the perfect day
And you sit alone with your thought
While the chimes ring out with a carol gay
For the joy that the day has brought."

Somehow these closing moments bring to my mind Carrie-Jacobs-Bond's folk song. Nelson Eddy, Mahalia Jackson and Paul Robeson all gave it a turn with their good voices, helping to fix it in our memories.

As I've embarked on this journey into the friendliness of the woods, I have done so to explore more deeply what I experienced in earlier years in scattered images in the woods, while pursuing a working life. Day by day, week by week, month by month, the journey has blended into a perfect day.

A day is a marvelous event.

I awake to a dawn. Whether it be sun or cloud, heat or cold, it is new. If I don't live in a smoggy city, I can deeply breathe in the fresh air and resolve to make the most of the day.

If I don't look too carefully, I can conclude that the day is like any other day, like a thousand days that have gone before this one. If I conclude that all things look the same, then I must find something to remind me that all things also change.

If I live on the 32nd story of a New York tenement building, I need to put a potted plant on my veranda or window sill; a little touch of the great changing out of doors, of the woods. It's a tonic for me.

That potted plant that helps me see changes needs to be a fast-growing bit of herbage, like an ivy, for we humans are an impatient lot. We love to make slams on nature, like saying something is so slow it is "like watching the grass grow." The ivy changes, reforms, expands, takes new shapes, and almost dances in front of me. If I see nothing else new about me, I can say something is new about this day.

When I sit in my wooly lawn chair, surrounded by brome grass and vividly blooming Canadian thistle that stands taller than my seated person, I am reminded that a month before it was little more than knee high. The change in a day is breathtaking at times.

When I began this sitting "journey" into the woods, I did not know if I would persist. What more was there to see from one week to another? Would a session or two tell it all?

At Home in the Woodlands

One experience that drew me on to answer that question was our family's 45 years spent in on wooded spot on Templar Point on the shores of Leech Lake. For one month a year, the family and I lived under canvas, cooked over open fires on raised log platforms called "altar fires," and ate on a log dining table. Although I didn't particularly look for it, the woods impressed upon me finally that even in that same spot, every year we saw something different.

I began to recount those changes. The American redstart had been plentiful in the late 1960s. A short time later he was gone.

Several small American elms graced the spot at first. Later, no elms. (Dutch elm disease?)

Several lovely small spruce trees grew up from saplings at the entrance to our outdoor "kitchen," nurtured by our coffee grounds. Later they disappeared.

To pump water, I had driven in the standpoint near a basswood sapling. I had to bend the sapling back a bit whenever I screwed on or off the pump. A foolish idea. You guessed it. Eventually, the sapling became too big and thick to bend, and I had to move the pump.

Yet, for all of that, some things surprisingly never seemed to change. That remains an awesome fact to me.

The single giant white pine in the center of that wooded plot on Templar Point never seemed to change. It was there and it was big when we arrived. It is there yet when we return to visit Templar Point today.

The giant cottonwood next to our "kitchen" cupboards was there when we came and is still there. I was always worried that some summer I would come back and find it crashed across the center of our "kitchen," but that didn't happen. The cottonwood was fast-growing enough so that I was aware that the bulk of its trunk increased with time.

Evening closes the perfect day. These last words become the evening of what I have to say.

Jacobs-Bond, the folk-song writer, said that the chimes ring out with a carol gay for the joy which the day has brought. She is right, in my case.

When evening came I became particularly aware of the chimes in the great bell-tower clock at Concordia College in Moorhead, Minnesota, across the Red River a mile from where I sat in the woods in North Dakota.

When I was writing near the river in Salzburg, Austria, suddenly at a certain evening hour the clock tower bells began going off all over the city. It was an absolutely marvelous celebration of the day.

I don't know for sure why I remark upon the chimes in the folk song. Perhaps it is because the end of a day is more than a phenomenon. It is celebratory. Such endings are times for chimes.

I have followed the pattern of the year in recounting the journey in the woods. I suppose that is natural, as that is how we see change happening in the short run.

In the long run, of course, it appears that the woods have not changed. I park my wooly chair under the big American elm in July. A year later, I park it there again. Unless I make a special effort, I do not consider the fact that every leaf on that tree was not there a year ago. The tree has changed.

Of course, I know that. And yet it is hard to get my mind around that fact. Every leaf being changed is too large a concept for my human reason.

That big elm was here by the Red River before I was born. It will still be here after I am gone.

Yet when my great, great grandson reads about that elm and comes back here, that elm will be gone and another tree (perhaps another elm) will have arisen in its place, and he will see it and remark, "Ah, there is the tree under which Grandfather sat!" It will seem to him that nothing has changed.

A day evolves into another day. A year evolves into another year. A life evolves into children and grandchildren.

The passing years invite me to move on. But, I do not like to move on. I like to put in anchors. I like to establish benchmarks. Perhaps that is because I have never been a refugee. Refugees live to see their home obliterated, to move on to another place, to become citizens of another country, and continue to live.

The woods teach me to move on, and to be happy with moving on. And in a strange and mystical sense they tell me they will always be with me. In Scotland, in Germany, in Canada, in Los Angeles, by northern lakes and Great Plains rivers — they will always be there in this mystical sense. Wherever I go, there will always be woods.

And if I stay in one spot on this planet and try to put down my anchors, the woods will change. They will not be the same woods next July that they are this July. If I can stay in one spot and learn that, I will have moved one inch in my understanding since the day when I was born. And that is cause to "let the chimes ring out with a carol gay."

Jacobs-Bond's song closes with talk of a friend we've made. Who is this person?

That, my friend, is you. You have taken the effort to read my words and to walk this journey with me. I have opened my life to you. Thank you for listening.

And yet, I do not know who you are. Someday, I would hope to meet you. You have a story to tell as well. You have a journey that you have taken of which you can speak. I would like to hear of it.

And on a Sunday evening, my grandnephew Michael taught me that in his area I would, among the ducks, most likely see the mallard, the wood duck, the bufflehead and the common merganser. So this old man continued the process of trying to wrap his mind around one more aspect of this wonderful world called "the woods."

Bibliography

Grant, John B., Our Common Birds and How to Know Them, Charles Scribner's Sons, New York, NY, 1891.f

Kricher, John C. and Gordon Morrison, A Field Guide to Ecology of Eastern Forests, Peterson Field Guides, Houghton Mifflin Company, Boston, MA, 1988.

Peterson, Roger Tory, Field Guide to the Birds (Eastern), Houghton Mifflin Company, Boston, MA, 1947.

About the author

James Alger, who lives in Fargo, N.D., has been a summer resident with his family in the lake country of northern Minnesota for over half a century. In that time, he has learned to love and appreciate the people and the woodlands of that area.

He first brought his family to Leech Lake when their youngest child was only six weeks old. They leased a lot on Templar Point from the Ojibwe people and settled in, determined to live outdoors for all of the summers they spent on the Point. At present, they summer on Ham Lake near Akeley, Minnesota, where Jim's father built a cabin in 1952. The cabin is primitive, and they are determined to keep it that way.

The family's Fargo home is near the Red River of the North. The woodland along the river bank is his favorite place for writing, when in Fargo.

Jim is a retired pastor of the Lutheran stripe. He and his family have served parishes in North Dakota, Minnesota, Iowa, Manitoba and the Yukon.

Made in the USA
Lexington, KY
16 July 2018